Battleground Europe
BATTLE OF THE BULGE

BASTOGNE

Cover painting by James Dietz, STOPPED COLD, M-4 Howitzer batteries at Bastogne hold off German tanks.

Battleground Europe
BATTLE OF THE BULGE

BASTOGNE

Michael Tolhurst

LEO COOPER

Published by
LEO COOPER
an imprint of
Pen & Sword Books Limited
47 Church Street, Barnsley, South Yorkshire S70 2AS
Copyright © Michael Tolhurst 2001

ISBN 0 85052 798 8

A CIP record of this book is available
from the British Library

Printed in the United Kingdom by
CPI UK

*For up-to-date information on other titles produced under the Leo Cooper
imprint, please telephone or write to:*

Pen & Sword Books Ltd, FREEPOST SF5, 47 Church Street
Barnsley, South Yorkshire S70 2BR
Telephone 01226 734555

CONTENTS

INTRODUCTION

It is hoped, with the aid of this book, that the reader will be helped to understand how the siege and relief of Bastogne in the cold December of 1944 came about. The Battle of the Ardennes, or as it came to be known, 'The Battle of the Bulge' (a term given by its characteristic shape formed by the German thrust through the Allied lines), was to become one of the greatest battles fought by the US Army in Europe. This, the last all out offensive initiative of the Second World War by the Germans, although brilliantly planned and executed, was to prove to be the beginning of the end for them in the West.

During the German drive west there were many actions fought in the Ardennes region, this book is about one of them.

This part of Europe is one of the most picturesque areas imaginable. High ridges and deep ravines abound in the area criss-crossed by fast flowing rivers and streams. Everywhere is covered with trees, many of them conifers. Main roads are few

The German frontier with Belgium showing the dragons teeth defences intended to stop tanks.

Concrete casemates provided strongpoints along the German West Wall. This one is draped with camouflage netting to conceal it from Allied aircraft.

and far between and generally follow the paths of the rivers through the valleys. On the Belgium-Luxembourg-German border the terrain is high and craggy. A volcanic ridge runs north to south just inside the German border and forms part of what the Germans call the Eifel Region. Winding itself through this is the River Our, which helps to make a natural barrier on Germany's frontier. This terrain stretches from Monschau in the north down to the River Moselle in the south. As if this was not a formidable barrier in itself, the Germans had constructed a line of defences along its borders from Holland down to the Swiss frontier. More than 3,000 concrete bunkers with interlocking fields of fire were built, along with anti-tank obstacles or dragons' teeth, forming a barrier across the open ground. The German propaganda machine proudly labelled the defences as the 'West Wall', however, the Allies referred to it as the – Siegfried Line.

Long before the war the Ardennes was a popular tourist area and people would visit to take in the breathtaking scenery, fill their lungs with the fresh air and of course sample the fine cuisine on offer. The same can be said for the Ardennes today, but now it has the added interest of being a battlefield that has changed little since the opposing armies slogged it out in that

bitter winter during the last few months of the Second World War.

Bastogne is, and was in 1944, a market town in southern Belgium standing behind the high ridges of the Eifel on a plateau surrounded by rolling hills. Much of the area is pasture land with interspersed woods made up mostly of conifers. Since the 15th Century the town has been famous for its smoked hams.

Looking at a map it is not difficult to see just how strategic the towns of Bastogne and St Vith were within the Ardennes region. They both held the key for the local road and rail network.

In the late Summer of 1944 the Allied armies had pursued retreating German formations through France, Belgium and Luxembourg and were poised to enter Germany. The next major task was to break through the West Wall and cross the River Rhine, a much respected natural obstacle. Supplies for the rapidly advancing armies were still being landed over the beaches of Normandy and ferried by vast convoys of trucks to the front lines hundreds of miles away. (These convoys were actually using more petrol than was being delivered). Although some seaports had been captured, the Germans had demolished most of the facilities before withdrawing. The port of Antwerp was the exception. It had been captured so quickly by the British in the beginning of September that the German defenders had had no time to set their demolition charges off. But the port was still closed to shipping, because the Germans controlled the Schelde Estuary, the entrance to Antwerp, from the Walcheren Islands. This was not opened for Allied shipping until the end of November.

With winter upon them, and with a lack of vital equipment, the Allies were slowing down. It was decided to halt and straighten the line, allowing the much needed supplies to catch up, and the weather to become more favourable in the spring of 1945 before beginning another offensive.

In and along the West Wall (breached in some places) the Allied troops dug in and made themselves as comfortable as possible. The Ardennes was one such area. The American First Army in this region had experienced bitter fighting around the border town of Aachen and had captured it in October. South of Aachen, in a heavily wooded area known as the Hurtgen Forest,

Fighting in the Hurtgen Forest was intense, the Germans putting up fierce resistance at this point on the border of the Third Reich.

division after division of American troops had been decimated. These weakened units, along with fresh divisions arriving from the United States, were sent to the Ardennes region. The battered formations to rest and take in replacements and the green divisions to become accustomed to front-line life. It became known as a 'Ghost Front', nothing much happened as both sides sent out patrols and went on to report back that all was quiet.

General Middleton's VIII Corps, of the 1st Army, occupied the area from just north of Losheim, right down south to the Luxembourg-French border. Along this line defending were, from north to south: the 14th Cavalry Group, 106th Infantry Division, 28th Infantry Division, a Combat Command from the 9th Armored Division and the 4th Infantry Division. These green or under-strength battle weary divisions were holding a line of about eighty-five miles – thus being grossly overstretched. Although the hilly terrain favoured the defender, they were hard pressed to adequately cover it.

As already stated, the two principal towns in the area were St Vith and Bastogne both being major hubs for the road and rail systems and both had railway stations. It was recognized that whoever had control of the two towns also had control of the road and rail network throughout the entire region.

Lieutenant General Hasso von Manteuffel, commander of the Fifth Panzer Army, along with two other armies, were massing undetected in and behind the dense Eifel region. He was well aware of the importance of the two towns and capture of St Vith and Bastogne featured on his list of objectives for the coming offensive.

The scene was set for one of the biggest battles of the Second World War. A battle of apparent surprise to the Allies and one that would finally be the undoing of Nazi Germany by expending virtually all of its reserves.

To say it was a complete surprise to the Allies would be wrong, prisoners had been taken by American patrols, these Germans had willingly told of a coming offensive. Certain tell-tale signs were there that the Germans were, even at this late stage in the conflict, considering going over to the offensive.

Front line GIs knew that something was up, but were told by 1st Army and Corps headquarters not to worry, 'Germany was finished, nothing's going to happen.' One man did heed all the warning signs, he was Colonel Benjamin A. 'Monk' Dickson of 1st Army Intelligence. Sifting through the reports coming in from the front line divisions he was convinced that the Germans were going to attack, he even thought the Ardennes would be the place. The hierarchy said he had been overworking and was making a mountain out of a mole hill and then promptly sent him on leave to Paris on 15 December 1944.

The peace and tranquility in the Ardennes was about to be shattered.

ACKNOWLEDGMENTS

I would like to take this opportunity for thanking all the people who helped me in writing this book, by remembering back and digging through their personal accounts and sharing their fears and thoughts with me. Especially, I really want to thank Professor Jim Thorpe from the University of Maryland and his researcher, Mike Basanta, for his tireless and outstanding work in obtaining the photographs from the US National Archives for this book. Also The Taylor Library for photographs.

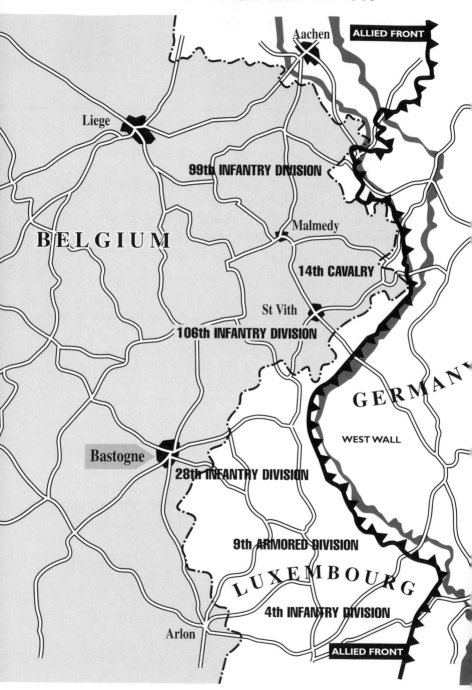

THE GHOST FRONT DECEMBER 1944

ALLIED FRONT

Aachen

Liege

99th INFANTRY DIVISION

Malmedy

BELGIUM

14th CAVALRY

St Vith

106th INFANTRY DIVISION

GERMANY

WEST WALL

Bastogne

28th INFANTRY DIVISION

9th ARMORED DIVISION

LUXEMBOURG

4th INFANTRY DIVISION

Arlon

ALLIED FRONT

GLOSSARY

AA **Anti Aircraft.**

AAA AW BN (SP) **Antiaircraft Artillery Automatic Weapons Battalion.** (Self-Propelled)

AB DIV **Airborne Division.** (12,979 men) Made up of three Parachute Infantry Regiments and one GliderInfantry Regiment.

AFAB **Armored Field Artillery Battalion.** Made up of 18 M7 self propelled 105mm Howitzers

AIB **Armored Infantry Battalion.** (Fully mechanised infantry carried in half-tracks)

AT **Anti-tank.**

BN **Battalion.** Approx 871 men

BAZOOKA **American hand held anti-tank Rocket.**

CCA **Combat Command A** ⎫ Three Combat
CCB **Combat Command B** ⎬ Commands make up an Armored
CCR **Combat Command Reserve** ⎭ Division

CP **Command Post**

13

CO	**Company.** Approx 193 men
DIV	**Division.** Approx 14,253 with 2,012 vehicles.
ENG	**Combat Engineer Battalion** (Approx 647 men)
FAB	**Field Artillery Battalion** (Approx 500 men split into 3 batteries.
GI	**Government Issue.** Anything Issued to the American Soldier, Including himself.
GIR	**Glider Infantry Regiment** Approx 2,980 men
GMC	**General Motors Corporation** 6x6 utility truck and was the workhorse of the US Army.
G3	**Corps and Divisional Operations Officer.**
HALF-TRACK	**An armored personnel carrier.** M2/M3 were the basic carriers. The M16 was based on the M3 and mounted four .50 machine guns.
INF	**Infantry.**
KAMPFGRUPPE	**German Combat Group** of variable sizes.
LUFTWAFFE	**German Airforce.**
PANZER	**German for Armour.** Eg tank. Panzergrenadiers = Armoured Infantry.

PANZER MKIV   Panzer Mark IV tank. Standard German tank with 75mm gun.

PANZERFAUST   German hand held Anti tank weapon.

PIR   **Parachute Infantry Regiment**
(Approx 2,370 men)

POW   **Prisoner of War**

REGT   **Regiment**

SHERMAN

Standard medium American Tank. Used by every Allied Nation. Crew of five, with a max Speed of 24 - 29 mph.There were many different variants, but most were armed with either a 75mm or 76mm gun.

STUART

American light tank. Crew of four. Max speed 36 mph. Armed with a 37mm gun and 2 .30 cal machine guns.

S2

Intelligence Officer of Regiment or lower

S3

Operations Officer of Regiment or lower.

| TD | **Tank Destroyer.** (Either the self-Propelled type, as in the M10 mounting a 3 inch gun, or the M18 armed with a 76mm gun. Also there was a towed type, a 3 inch field gun, drawn by a vehicle. |

| TF | **Task Force** |

| TIGER | **German tank.** Mounting a 88mm gun. Weighing 56 tons it was an awesome predator. |

| T/SGT | **Technical Sergeant.** A rank in the US Army. 'T'denotes a qualified skill e.g radio operator, etc. |

17

USAAF	**United States Army Air Force.**
VGD	**Volksgrenadier Division.** Came into being late in the war. Made up of fillers from the Navy/Air-Force and mixed with regular Army. (Even so, some proved to be effective fighting units).
NEBELWERFER	**German multi-barrelled mortar.**

88   German 88mm gun.
                            Much feared by the Allies.
                            It was mounted on Tiger
                            Tanks, or as a field piece
                            In either the ground or anti-
                            Aircraft role.

CHAPTER ONE

HITLER'S PLAN

In the *Wolfsschanze* (Wolf's Lair), Hitlers headquarters at Rastenburg, situated in a forest in East Prussia, the daily conference was filled with an air of doom and gloom. That Saturday, 16 September 1944, it was reported that the Allies had gained a toe hold on German soil. The once all-victorious German fighting machine had been pushed back to its homeland. On the Eastern Front the Russian summer offensive had reached the borders of East Prussia. The losses in manpower and materials had been colossal.

The conference had adjourned when Hitler called his four highest military advisers into another room. First in, was Field Marshal Wilhelm Keitel, Supreme Commander of all German Armies, closely followed by, General Alfred Jodl, chief of the German Operations Staff, Heinz Guderian, the famous tank commander now Commander of the Eastern Front, and General

The German plan.

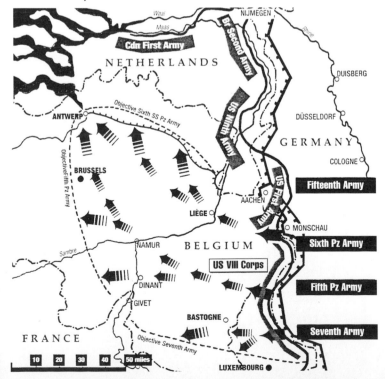

Kreipe, representing an absent Air Marshal Goring, head of the Luftwaffe (German airforce).

Alfred Jodl went on to tell Hitler about the steadily mounting Allied divisions that were now knocking on Germany's door. Obviously none of these subjects pleased the Führer. Suddenly, Hitler interrupted Jodl, pointed to the laid out map before him and said 'I have just made a momentous decision. I shall go over to the counter-attack, here out of the Ardennes, with the objective – Antwerp.'

The room was shocked into silence. Had the bomb attack back in July finally taken its toll? Hitler had been left both emotionally and physically injured after the assassination attempt on his life. A bomb had been planted in a room during one of his meetings, but he had escaped serious injury.

Hitler's enthusiasm reminded his staff of the heady *Blitzkrieg* days of 1940. He went on to rightly surmise that the Allied supply lines were stretched to the limit, and that the steam had finally run out of the lightning pursuit to the German border. His plan was simple, he would attack out of the Ardennes, known to his intelligence services as a soft spot, and drive for the recently captured port of Antwerp, thus forming a wedge,

Hitler's plan was to strike at a vulnerable section of the Allied Front. American GIs of the 28th DIV queue at the rest centre in Clervaux unaware of the pending onslaught.

between the forces of the United States and the British and Canadian armies fighting in the north, thus splitting the Allies in half. He knew that the two sides opposing him were prone to disagreement and that the alliance was considered to be shaky. Driving a wedge might well cause the Anglo/American team to fall out. Then Hitler could sue for peace under his own terms and turn his full attention to what he considered to be the greater threat – the Russians.

To the men present, this was the old Hitler again, full of energy and new ideas. The attack was provisionally set for 1 November 1944. The officers present were then sworn to secrecy with threats to their own, and their family's lives.

On 25 September, Jodl was ordered by Hitler to start making the necessary plans for the new counter-attack. Field Marshall Keitel was given the task of organizing the fuel and ammunition that would be needed, and to report when it could be expected to be ready. General Rudolf Gercke, Chief of Transportation, was brought

Generaloberst **Alfred Jodl.**

into the plan. Hitler ordered the formation of a new army especially for the attack; it was to be named the Sixth Panzer Army. He entrusted his great friend, General Josef 'Sepp' Dietrich to be its commander. All its armoured divisions were to be made up of Waffen SS.

Even though the Allied airforce was bombing the industrial heart of Germany round the clock, actual wartime production was reaching an all time high. Manpower for the coming offensive was to be a problem, but was soon overcome when the enlisting age was changed to between sixteen and sixty. Originally it had been eighteen and fifty. Both civilian and military offices were combed of non-important administrative personnel, and finally redundant sailors and airmen who had neither ships nor aircraft were thrown into the army to form the new divisions so badly needed. Hitler called them *Volksgrenadiers* (People's Infantry).

Badge of the 77th Regiment, 26th *Volksgrenadiers*, with Köln Cathedral as emblem.

These new divisions would be smaller than the usual complement for Wehrmacht divisions, but to make up for this, more men would be armed with automatic weapons and

Panzerfausts, (hand held, rocket firing anti-tank weapon). The Panther and Tiger tanks that were rolling off the assembly lines were given straight to the new Panzer Brigades being formed.

The Allies had air superiority, which worried the generals, but Hitler's answer was that the offensive would take place in either November or December when the usual bad weather would ground the dreaded Allied fighter-bombers.

The coming attack would be led by Field Marshal Gerd von Rundstedt, who had been out of favour with the Führer due to the failure of the German forces in repelling the Allied invasion. However, Hitler realized Rundstedt would be good for the job and would perhaps revive the flagging German Army.

Generalfeldmarsch
Gerd von Rundste

By early October General Gercke was well ahead of his schedule; Rhine bridges were reinforced to carry the new seventy-ton King Tiger; ferries were adapted to carry locomotives and tanks; rail tracks were laid across some road

New Tiger IIs (*Königstiger*) being reviewed prior to the German offensive in the West.

bridges; makeshift bridging spans were constructed and hidden along the eastern banks in case the permanent bridges were bombed.

On 11 October Jodl went back to Hitler and submitted his plan which he code-named CHRISTROSE. Three armies totalling twelve panzer and eighteen infantry divisions would advance on a broad front, crossing the River Meuse by the second day and reaching Antwerp after one week. Hitler sent him away to do some fine tuning.

The following day Keitel released a message to all commanders on the Western Front, knowing full well that it would be intercepted by the Allies, to the effect that no counter-offensive was possible and that all forces must be deployed for imminent defence of the Fatherland. This, it was hoped by the German High Command, would explain to Allied Intelligence why there was a build up of forces and a flurry of activity behind the German line.

Jodl returned to Hitler with the revised plan on 21 October and Hitler was delighted, giving it his seal of approval. He renamed the planned operation WACHT AM RHEIN (Watch on the Rhine). A code name that would suggest a defensive plan.

That same day Hitler summoned to the *Wolfsschanze*, SS-*Sturmbannführer* Otto Skorzeny, a giant of a man with blond hair, who like Hitler was Austrian. In 1943 Skorzeny had rescued the Italian Dictator, Mussolini, from the Allies. More recently he had led a raid on the seat of the Hungarian Government in Budapest kidnapping the Hungarian leader's son to stop that nation's defection from the Axis forces.

SS-Sturmbannführer Otto Skorzeny.

Hitler listened intently to Skorzeny's accounts, and then went on to tell him the details of WACHT AM RHEIN. Skorzeny was to form a special brigade of German troops that could converse in English and would be wearing and using captured American equipment. The brigade was to go ahead of the attacking armies, and capture key bridges over the Meuse River. The brigade, operating in small units, would ultimately create havoc behind the American lines. Hitler added 'I know you will do your best' and promoted him then and there to *Obersturmbannführer* (Lieutenant Colonel).

Jodl, Hitler and Keitel the three men who devised and planned Operation WACHT AM RHEIN.

Hardly had Skorzeny set about forming the special unit titled, 'Panzer Brigade 150' when he came across a circular which compromised the secret operation. Keitel had signed, and by so doing, authorized the document which asked for volunteers, who could speak English, for a special mission and that successful applicants would join a new unit under the command of Skorzeny. Further, that all captured American equipment was to be handed in. He was furious and quite rightly surmised that this order was bound to fall into the hands of the Allies. But in case Hitler himself found out about this breech of secrecy, Skorzeny was ordered to go on with his part of the plan.

On 22 October, Hitler finally decided to tell Rundstedt and also Field Marshal Walter Model, Commander of Army Group B, whose actual troops would carry the offensive.

Their Chief of Staffs were called to the *Wolfsschanze*.

Generalfeldmarschall **Walter Model.**

Representing Rundstedt's was Lieutenant General Siegfried Westphal, and attending for Model was Lieutenant General Hans Krebs. Both men were flabbergasted when the outlines of the plan was presented to them. Hitler went on to promise them 1,500 planes, which would be on hand for the attack. Keitel explained that sufficient ammunition and gasoline would be made available. Westphal and Krebs rushed back to their respective headquarters to inform their Field Marshals of the plan.

Rundstedt called it 'A stroke of genius' but thought it a little ambitious with what was on hand. Model, as blunt as ever, reacted by saying 'This plan hasn't got a damned leg to stand on.' Both began work on a version of their own, ones that were on a smaller scale, with the idea of destroying the American divisions around the Aachen area. The plans were submitted to Hitler who immediately threw them out; his original idea was to stand. In the meantime the offensive was postponed, even the ambitious Hitler realized, he had not given himself enough time to gather his forces together.

Huge deception plans were initiated, forces were built up in front of the Aachen area to suggest a huge defensive operation to try and prevent the Americans crossing the Rhine from there. In the meantime, where massive forces were assembling in the Ardennes, the front went silent. Trains were used at night to bring up the mass of troops, vehicles and supplies needed. All these were hidden in the dense forests just east of the front lines. Supply problems prompted Hitler to cancel the operation several more times, although he was not unduly worried as even worse weather was predicted for mid December. Finally, 16 December was to be the day, Zero Hour was fixed for 0530.

Obergruppenführer Josef 'Sep' Dietrich.

Generalleutnant **Erich Brandenberger.**

eneralleutnant **asso von Manteuffel.**

Final plans were worked out, the main attack, would be carried by Dietrich's Sixth Panzer Army. This would break through the northern sector of the Ardennes, head northwest, cross the Meuse River and drive all out for Antwerp. Immediately south of the Sixth, Lieutenant General Hasso von Manteuffel with his Fifth Panzer Army was to surround the Schnee Eifel, a prominent height salient occupied by the US 106th Infantry Division and capture the town of

Generaloberst Walter Krüger.

St Vith. Also in his assigned area he was to capture the other important town of Bastogne. After which the Fifth would head for Brussels and then Antwerp protecting Dietrich's left flank. Meanwhile Lieutenant General Erich Brandenberger's Seventh Army was to protect the flank of the other two from possible American interventions from the south.

This particular area of the Ardennes had been carefully selected, because, it was known to be thinly defended. The American troops there were either new to combat or were sent to this 'quiet area' to rest and train replacements after a mauling elsewhere. The heavily wooded terrain made it ideal to conceal large amounts of men and their equipment, and along with this, the Germans knew just about every position and bunker, for they themselves had been in exactly the same positions three months before.

Manteuffel set to work organizing his Fifth Panzer Army. He understood armoured warfare very well, he had been an officer in the pre-war panzer troops. His bravery and leadership in Russia and North Africa had seen him climb the ladder of military success from divisional commander straight to an army command.

His plan was for *Generaloberst* Walter Krüger's LVIII Panzer Corps to cross the Our River either side of Ouren, attack towards Houffalize and form a bridgehead over the Meuse River in the vicinity of Namur.

To *General der Panzertruppen* Heinrich Freiherr von Lüttwitz and his XLVII Corps he gave orders that he was to cross the Our at Dasburg and Gemund,

General Heinrich von Lüttwitz.

26

head west through Clervaux and capture the all-important road centre of Bastogne, then 'drive like hell' for the Meuse, crossing south of Namur.

XLVII Corps was comprised of the 26th *Volksgrenadier* Division, 2nd Panzer Division and the Panzer Lehr Division. The 26th *Volksgrenadier* Division (VGD) had been fighting constantly on the Russian Front since 1941. It was brought back and made up to strength with replacements mostly from the navy. Commanded by *Generalmajor* Heinz Kokott, the Division consisted of the 78th Regiment, 77th Regiment and the 39th Fusilier Regiment and was garrisoning a section of the West Wall immediately opposite the US 28th Division.

Generalmajor Kokott.

The 2nd Panzer Division, under Colonel Meinrad von Lauchert, was a crack unit that had been fighting all the way back from Normandy. It had suffered heavily and what was left of it was made good with quality troops from Austria. It was issued with the modern Panther tank, which had a new revolutionary infrared sight fitted.

General Meinrad von Lauchert.

Panzer Lehr Division, under *Generalleutnant* Fritz Bayerlein, had been involved in heavy fighting with Patton's US 3rd Army in the Saar region and it too had suffered badly. It never did get up to full strength again. To make up this loss two battalions of tank destroyers and an assault gun brigade were given to Panzer Lehr prior to the attack.

The latest equipment was issued to Panzer Lehr's reconnaissance battalion,

Generalleutnant Fritz Bayerlein.

which, along with the reconnaissance battalion of the 26th VGD would spearhead the attack.

To further strengthen XLVII Corps, Manteuffel gave Lüttwitz the 15th Volks Werfer Brigade, the 766th Volks Artillery Corps, the 600th Army Engineer Battalion and the 182nd Flak Regiment. Coupled with this all three divisions were reinforced with additional self-propelled assault guns. Also two 60-ton bridges were earmarked for the Corps to enable its heavy Panthers to ford the rivers.

Although air support was promised both Kokott and Lüttwitz were sceptical, as they had been let down too many times in the past and so were just glad of impending bad weather and night time operations. They were also reassured by the vast amount of flak guns that were being made available for the coming attack.

If all went well the 26th VGD would force a crossing of the Our and Clerf Rivers on the left of the Corps and hold the area open for the armour of 2nd Panzer Division. Panzer Lehr Division would follow and overtake the infantry division in the

The crossing point on the river Our of the 26th Volksgrenadier Division.

The bridge across the River Our at Gemünd today.

race for Bastogne. When Bastogne was reached the infantry of the 26th VGD would occupy the town and provide cover on the left flank while the panzers crossed the Meuse River.

By 11 December the build up was complete, the German rail network (*Reichsbahn*) had worked miracles in getting everything and everybody to where they were supposed to be. Hitler moved his headquarters to a bunker complex at Wiesental. Just two kilometres to the south was the castle of Ziegenberg, at Bad Nauheim, which was the headquarters of *Oberkommando* West.

On 13 December the last of the reports came in to Hitler's headquarters: Keitel reported that petrol was on hand, each tank would have enough to travel about ninety to one hundred miles; eight days' worth of ammunition was at the front with another eight days' supply held in reserve; the Luftwaffe had over 300 aircraft ready, many of which were the new Messerschmitt 262 jets.

The following night the armies moved their attacking forces up to within three miles of the front line. To muffle out the sound to the unsuspecting Americans, planes flew up and down the front and straw was strewn across roads to dampen the noise of tracks and wheels

During the night of 15 December Lüttwitz moved his assault divisions up to their start lines. The 26th VGD were already in position, as its 78th Regiment had been defending that particular sector of the West Wall. It had outposts across the

River Our, which Kokott had manned at night. This night he sent the whole regiment across. To the Americans high on Skyline Drive nothing would seem unusual about the movement below them. Gradually, an increasing number of *Volksgrenadiers* were put across the river by inflatable rubber boats until most of the division was within a few minutes' walk from one of the Americans' Outposts.

Kokott's initial plan for the 26th VGD was for its 77th Regiment to form on the right near Hosingen with the 39th slightly to it's left and rear. The 77th would cut round north of Hosingen and dash straight for the River Clerf bridges at Drauffelt. The 39th would cut across country and seize the road

junction and bridges at Wilwerwiltz on the Clerf. These objectives were to be secured by nightfall on the 16th.

Unteroffizier Ludwig Lindemann was serving in the command position of *Kompanietruppenführer* [Company/Troop Leader] with the 10th Kompanie, 77th Infanterie Regiment.

'*Our unit was stationed in Übereisenbach and our Kompaniegefechtstab* [Company Command HQ] *was in the first bunker on the right hand side of the street above the Theis Inn. Our officer, Leutnant Gerlach, three runners and I, as Kompanietruppenführer, lived in the bunker. To begin with life on the frontier was peaceful and apart from patrol activity, terrain reconnaissance and the training of the men in new infantry weapons nothing much was happening. Supply line for the 10th Companie, IR 77, was based on a farm back in Karlshausen under the command of Hauptfeldwebel* [Quartermaster], *Karl Hans, who was an extremely popular non-commissioned officer.*

Unteroffizier **Ludwig Lindemann.**

'*At a battalion briefing at the beginning of December we were informed that on the 16th of that month we would be the lead unit in a big westerly offensive involving a great number of divisions. Our main goal was to be Bastogne in Belgium. We belonged to the 5th Panzer Army and our Divisional*

Commander was Generalmajor Kokott.

'Patrols had scouted out and established the final assembly areas for the coming attack. The previous month, November, a raiding patrol from our company had been ordered to enter the enemy lines in an attempt to capture prisoners. Leutnant Gerlach, Obergefreiter Erwin Blankenberg, who was our dispatch rider, and eight men were to set off at midnight and patrol in the vicinity of Putscheid in Luxembourg.

'The men formed up on the street which led north to the village of Putscheid. After passing through the woods separating the American and German positions they proceeded slowly and carefully into Putscheid itself, using the buildings on the left-hand side of the road for cover. Blankenberg, was leading, closely followed by two grenadiers, and behind them was Leutnant Gerlach and the rest of the patrol. When they were just past the first houses a machine gun opened up on them. Immediately Blankenberg dropped with two shots in the head. One of the two with him went to drag him to cover but saw that he was dead and himself became wounded. Leutnant Gerlach had been caught in the same burst of fire, taking hits in the chest, and was also killed. The remaining members of the raiding patrol, amongst them two wounded, beat a retreat to the north-west and cover.

Piles of artillery munitions being stocked for the coming battle.

'In the morning they arrived at Company HQ and reported the outcome of the raid. This I immediately passed onto Battalion HQ. The Company was now without a commissioned officer, therefore I assumed command as Kompanietruppenführer, until a replacement arrived. If my memory serves me right the new officer was called Bremke. He had no combat experience.

'At midnight on 15 December 1944, it began. Moving off in squads we reached the River Our which marked the frontier boundary. Then, as quietly as we could, we doubled up the bank of the river in a northerly direction. We crossed the Our on a narrow plank and came to our assigned assembly point – we were probably below Hosingen. It was 3 am by the time we started regrouping and we were all frozen. The platoons and squads were assigned to their sectors in readiness for the coming attack. It wasn't permitted to smoke in case the enemy saw the glare of the cigarette. We could only move about carefully and talk in whispers. We had no idea of the whereabouts of the American outpost positions. We later learned that there were no frontline positions in that particular area where we attacked. As far as one could observe it was still peaceful all along the front.'

Colonel Hurley Fuller.

Immediately in front of the 26th VGD was the 110th Regiment of the US 28th Infantry Division. This American division was in the sector for a rest and to absorb replacements after a gruelling fight in the Hurtgen Forest. A rest centre had been set up in Clervaux where men came from the division on three day visits. Bathing facilities and clean uniforms were available. The GIs could take in a movie, drink beer, even though it was on the weak side, and get coffee and doughnuts from the American Red Cross. Here also, set in the Hotel Claravallis was the Command Post of the 110th Regiment. Its commander was Colonel Hurley Fuller.

The 110th Regt was in the centre of the Division with its two sister regiments either side, the 112th Regt to the north and the 109th Regt to the south. Of the 110th's three battalions only the

The Hotel Claravallis in Clervaux. This served as the Command Post for the 28th Division's 110th Regiment.

Vehicles of Panzer Lehr Division on the move in December 1944.

1st and 3rd battalions were actually in the line, the 2nd Battalion was in the rear, in the village of Donnange, and was marked as divisional reserve.

The 1st and 3rd Battalions had no way of making a continuous defence line in their nine to ten mile front. Instead they defended villages in about rifle company strength. These villages were situated on a ridge line, between the Our and Clerf Rivers along which runs a north-south road connecting St Vith with Diekirch. This road became known to the Americans as 'Skyline Drive'. The roads and villages were between one and a half to two miles from the River Our.

Outposts were set up between the ridge and the river, but were only manned during daylight hours. At night German and American patrols stalked each other – that's if they ever made contact in the vast wooded area. In this sector, there were four roads that ran from the German border (The Our River), up and over 'Skyline Drive' and on into Clervaux. It was at these points where the roads crossed the ridge that the US 110th Regiment concentrated its forces. Only the most northerly road at Marnach was of any real use for it had a good hard surface and ran through Clervaux and on to Bastogne. It was this road that the Germans had decided to use for their main drive, and it would be connected to their own roads on the German side of the border by bridging the river at Dasburg. The other three roads, although inferior, were going to be used by the 26th VGD once the bridge was in at Gemünd.

The engineers in this sector began constructing the bridge during the night, but leading units of 2nd Panzer Division at 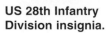Dasburg faced a delay. The road leading to the demolished bridge site was blocked by huge iron gates which were a part of the West Wall defences, and nobody could find the keys. They would have to be blown up, but as that would doubtless alert the attention of the Americans, it would have to wait for the opening barrage to commence in order to cover the sound of the demolition explosions.

The clock ticked on – H-Hour approached.

**US 28th Infantry
Division insignia.**

CHAPTER TWO

ATTACK

At precisely 05.30 on 16 December 1944, the massed guns and Werfers opened up. All hell was let loose along the front. The artillery was extremely accurate and immediately communication lines were severed. Shells rained down on the American positions and Clervaux was saturated with rockets.

Cursing men half asleep, in the area for a supposed rest, spilled from their beds totally unaware of what was going on. Colonel Fuller was one of these men. He rushed downstairs to his operations room, just off the hotel lobby, only to be told that all communication to his front line units were out, and worse still, contact had been lost with General Norman D Cota at Divisional Headquarters in the town of Wiltz, seven miles southwest of them.

Along Skyline Drive, the 26th VGD were in and around the Americans before they realized what was going on. The thick fog early that morning made it difficult to determine who was friend or foe.

THE GERMAN BREAKTHROUGH

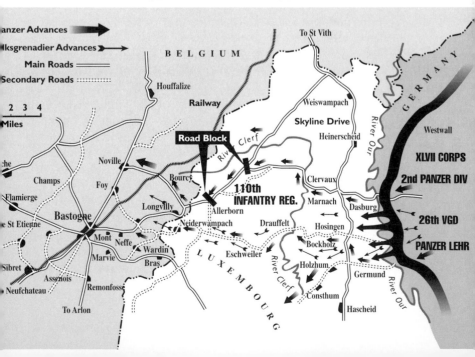

Ludwig Lindemann

'It was still dark when, at 5 am, a mighty drumfire of artillery, smoke-shell mortars, multiple rocket launchers and anti-aircraft guns suddenly opened up. We could see the land in front of our sector, near Hosingen, erupting with explosions. One had the impression that the whole world was going under. Such a massive and unrelenting drumfire I had never experienced before.

'One of the first salvos fell short and we suffered our first casualties – from our own guns. We had one dead and a few injured. The VB (artillery spotter) for our attached artillery was positioned near me; he immediately had the firing stopped in our sector, giving fresh co-ordinates. The barrage began to come down further forward.

'There was much apprehension among the men as we awaited the order to move forward into the blackness before us, which was being punctuated by bright flashes of exploding ordnance. Suddenly, behind us, searchlights shone against the sky, reflecting against the low clouds, thus lighting up the whole battlefield and surroundings. A shout resounded: "Company to attack, forward march!" Half crouched, instinctively presenting a smaller target, we cautiously began moving forwards, up the sloping terrain. Thank goodness we didn't strike any minefields here. In a short time we arrived at the first houses of Hosingen, and opened fire at windows and doors. We had surprised a few of them in their sleep and at the far end of the village I could see American soldiers running from the houses. I even saw one of them in his underwear. Our Company had successfully captured the southern part of Hosingen. Behind the village our 10th Company regrouped and awaited further orders.'

The defenders of Marnach and part of Hosingen held their ground but were only too aware that German troops had already passed either side of them and were proceeding down the reverse slope of Skyline Drive. Back at the River Our the German engineers were feverishly erecting the bridges needed to get the panzers across.

Although Germans were passing through the thin line of defence quite easily, the two main villages atop the ridge held out. Without capturing the villages of Hosingen and Marnach the two main routes from the bridges remained closed. At Hosingen the aggressiveness of the attack faltered, much to

36

German artillery firing at night.

Volksgrenadiers during their advance.

Generalmajor Kokott's disgust, and at Marnach to the north the leading battalion from the 2nd Panzer Division had run into an American minefield. It delayed them so much that it was now fully light and the covering fog had lifted. The Germans attacked in strength but were held back by Company B and a platoon of towed anti-tank guns from the US 630th Tank Destroyer Battalion.

Just after 09.00 that morning the communication lines began to work again. Fuller telephoned Cota requesting that his 2nd Battalion, which was held in reserve, be sent forward to aid his other two battalions. Cota refused his request on the grounds that the situation had not developed enough to warrant committing his only reserve force. But, knowing that the 110th's area was the most critical, he sent two companies of medium tanks from the 707th Tank Battalion (thirty-four Sherman tanks) to their aid.

On the arrival of the Shermans Fuller sent the tankers out piecemeal to different places to help the hard pressed infantry. He kept one platoon with him in Clervaux, and sent two platoons to Marnach. Other infantry from Company B's 1st Battalion had tried to reach them but had been beaten back by the German tide. The Shermans made Marnach and cleared the southern approaches, one platoon was then sent back to help in the defence of another village whilst the other platoon of tanks

German infantry crossing a river barrier during the Ardennes offensive.

Tankers from CCB 10th Armoured Division take a break on their way to Bastogne.

was to move south along Skyline Drive and sweep the Germans from it as far as Hosingen. This they did quite successfully, and were relieved to find Hosingen still in the hands of Company K. Also, about a mile south of Hosingen at a crossroads marked by a café (Café Schincker) a small platoon of men held out. These, and the two villages of Consthum and Holtzhum were now the only places held firmly by the 110th Regiment, but ammunition was getting low, they could not hold indefinitely.

Meanwhile the German engineers were still trying to erect the bridges, it was hard going, everything had to be done manually, and to compound the problems the Our River was flowing fast and deep due to heavy rain and melting snow.

Early afternoon and the bridge in the 2nd Panzer Division's area at Dasburg was completed. The first panzers began to rumble across. It was not long before a tank approaching the bridge misjudged a sharp turn and crashed into one of the spans. There followed another couple of hours of repair work, by which time the engineers at Gemünd had completed their bridge.

The Germans now renewed their attacks with even more

force. Now that the bridges were open, self-propelled guns and tanks could be brought into use against the stubborn villages.

Shortly after dark Marnach became the centre of attention. Company B held out for as long as it could. When it became known that the Germans were renewing their attack supported by machinegun-firing half-tracks the American defence finally collapsed.

That evening General Cota contacted Fuller to say that he was now releasing his reserve troops and that he had also released a company of light tanks held in the 112th Infantry Regiment area to the north. They were proceeding south to retake Marnach. Acting on this information Fuller immediately set to work to organize a plan for the next day. Both the 2nd Infantry Battalion and the company of tanks would combine for an attack on Marnach. What the American Commander did not know was that the town was already in German hands. At the very time that the American plan was being formulated panzers were assembling in Marnach ready for a big push on to Clervaux with its two important bridges over the Clerf.

General Heinrich von Lüttwitz

'On 16 December, in the morning, an attack was ordered with 2nd Panzer Division on the right flank, 26th Volksgrenadier Division on the left flank and Panzer Lehr Division in reserve. On 17 December 1944, Panzer Lehr Division moved in front of 26th Volksgrenadier Division. The engineer units of 26th Volksgrenadier Division had completed the necessary bridging to enable Panzer Lehr Division to break through, and it was hoped to push on to the town with this fast moving unit.'

General Fritz Bayerlein

'In the original plan, 26th Volksgrenadier Division was to take the crossings over the Our, then those over the Clerf, and establish bridgeheads. Only after this would parts of Panzer Lehr Division thrust west toward Bastogne over the Drauffelt Bridgehead (south of Clervaux). As the attack of the 26th Volksgrenadier Division against Drauffelt did not succeed quickly and the American resistance in Hosingen and Bockholz on 16 December 1944 could not be crushed, units of Panzer Lehr Division, on orders from higher headquarters, were committed against Holtzhum and Consthum to win the Kautenbach

To support the advance German engineers hastily threw bridges across rivers, railway cuttings and other obstacles.

bridgehead, and from there to push on to the west. The Panzer Reconnaissance Battalion was committed first and, later 901st Panzer Grenadier Regiment also was committed. The Panzer Reconnaissance Battalion took Holtzhum, while 901st Panzer Grenadier Regiment attacked Consthum, which was doggedly defended. During this attack, 26th Volksgrenadier Division succeeded in capturing Drauffelt on 17 December 1944. On orders from higher headquarters, the attack of 901st Panzer Grenadier Regiment was immediately discontinued, and the Regiment also moved through the Drauffelt bridgehead in order that a divisional attack could be launched against Bastogne.

In general, the plan was to thrust forward where it could be done quickest and easiest, and to commit our troops at the first point we succeeded in establishing a bridgehead over the Clerf.'

At the end of the day, the Germans had not achieved their initial objectives, this was mainly due to the hold ups on the bridging, and the tenacity and aggression on the part of the defending G.I. But they were well situated for the following day's drive.

That Saturday morning the Supreme Commander, General Dwight D. Eisenhower had attended the wedding of his orderly Mickey McKeough. That day he had also learned that he had been promoted to Five Star General – a day for celebration. The only thing marring it so far was the news that the band leader

A .30 caliber machine gunner awaits the onslaught.

Glenn Miller was overdue on his flight to France.

That afternoon in his headquarters at Versailles the Supreme Commander was holding a meeting with General Omar Bradley about infantry replacements for the depleted divisions. The meeting was interrupted with the news of the German attack.

Although the initial objectives of the Germans were not then realized, it was obvious that Middleton's VIII Corps was being hit hard. Reserves and reinforcements would have to be sent. Bradley telephoned General Patton, who was in his Third Army's HQ at Nancy, and told him to release the 10th Armored Division and move it up to Luxembourg City. George Patton bitterly protested as he needed it for his offensive in the Saar region, but was quickly overruled and told curtly that 'Ike was running the war not him'.

CHAPTER THREE

BREAKTHROUGH

By dawn on the morning of 17 December the Germans had advanced eight miles west from their river crossings at Dasburg and Gemünd. Small groups of Volksgrenadiers had reached the outskirts of Clervaux and were firing small arms into the town. Fuller sent tanks to relieve his now surrounded outposts, but the tanks were forced back by superior German forces with heavy losses.

At 11.30 Fuller made a call to Cota demanding more reinforcements,

'I need more artillery support, more tanks.'

'I'll send you a battery of self-propelled guns and that's all I can spare. I've got two other regiments screaming for help.'

Fuller shouted down the phone again

'And we've got twelve Tigers sitting on the high ground east of town, looking down our throats.'

'Sorry Fuller, one battery is all I can give you,

**Major General
Norman Cota**

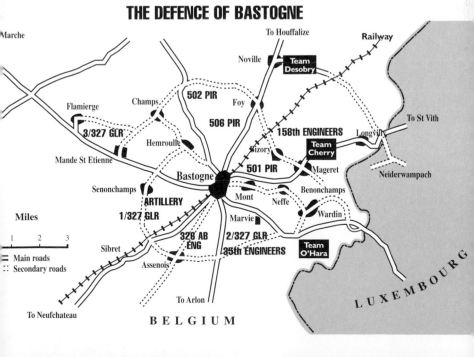

THE DEFENCE OF BASTOGNE

remember your orders hold at all costs. No retreat, nobody comes back.'

Silence fell on the conversation.

'Do you understand, Fuller?'

'Yes sir, nobody comes back,' the Colonel replied.

By mid afternoon German forces had just about encircled the men in Clervaux and Panzers were beginning to enter the town from three directions.

The US 110th's 2nd Battalion which was due to attack Marnach that morning had, at 0730, run straight into the 2nd Panzer Division coming down the road from that village. Although it battled bravely against the superior fire-power it soon succumbed to the might of the German panzers.

The attack south into Marnach by the light M5 Stuart tanks along Skyline Drive was a complete disaster. The tanks were funnelled into a narrow road and were forced to advance in column. As they exited the village of Heinerscheid German 88mm guns began to pick them off one by one. It was like a shooting gallery, within ten minutes eight tanks had been destroyed by gunfire, three more were hit by Panzerfausts. Clervaux was now in serious danger of being captured. Fuller sent a platoon of tanks from the 707th Tank Battalion up the twisting road to the east. At the top of the hill the Shermans hit head on with the German advanced guard. Three Shermans and

Panzer MkIVs advancing during the breakthrough.

88mm firing in the ground role against tanks.

four Mk IV Panzers were destroyed.

The Germans were taken aback and their assault was stalled momentarily. The road into Clervaux became blocked with burning tanks belonging to both sides. The village of Hosingen was still being firmly held by Company K, but this village lay astride one of the roads much needed by Kokott's 26th VGD. There was a bottleneck beginning to build up and the German transport started to tail back. Kokott ordered that Hosingen was to be bypassed and by the afternoon the Germans had secured bridgeheads over the River Clerf in at least four places, one of which was at Drauffelt.

Ludwig Lindemann of the 26th VGD:

'During the Ardennes Offensive our battle commander was Hauptmann Josef Raab who had been awarded the Iron Cross on the Eastern Front for his bravery in connection with the defence of the Weichselbrückenkopf [bridgehead] near Pulawi. With our sixty-five-man combat group under his command he had prevented Russian troops from breaking through. With him in command of our company we felt confident.

'The 77th Regiment and the 39th Fusilier Regiment of the 26th Volksgrenadier Division, had taken the Americans by surprise and opened up the route to the west. After heavy resistance by the enemy in the town of Hosingen our division

*succeeded in surrounding the whole town. We in the 2nd
Battalion had to fight for every cellar and every garden wall. At
midday, 18 December 1944, the Americans surrendered and we
took sixteen Officers and three hundred and sixty-five men
prisoner. Seven tanks were destroyed and a lot of war material
was captured. This action opened the route to Bastogne.*

*But what started as a military success would end in streams
of blood. Today the cemeteries of that region speak loud and clear
of what awaited our troops.'*

Leading elements of Panzer Lehr Division, with the
Reconnaissance Battalion from the 26th VGD, were already
moving west towards the all-important town of Bastogne.

General Heinrich von Lüttwitz:

*'The northern bridgeheads across the Clerf and the Our rivers
had been built by 2 Panzer Division. These were the bridgeheads
which controlled the movement of infantry on to the Longvilly
road. The two lower bridgeheads, built by the 26th
Volksgrenadier Division engineers over the same streams, made
possible the sweep against the lines of communication south of
Bastogne and the attack against the town from that direction.
The dividing line between 2 Panzer Division and Panzer Lehr
Division for the attack against Bastogne was on an east to west
line about halfway between Noville and Bastogne. The objective
of 2 Panzer Division was the road junction at Herbaimont
northwest of Bastogne near Tenneville. The mission of Panzer
Lehr Division was to take Bastogne from the south. This was the
initial plan contained in the original order for the Ardennes
attack.'*

Because of the worrying situation in the US VIII Corps sector
the principal strategic reserve force of north-west
Europe was to be released. This consisted of the 82nd
and 101st Airborne Divisions. Both divisions were
in the Rheims area of France busily refitting after
their recent battles in Holland during Operation
MARKET GARDEN. The men were there, letting
off steam and the rivalry between the two
divisions was immense, it did not take much
provocation to start the two sides swinging fists at
each other. During the evening of 17 December they
were given their orders. It was so sudden a move that

VIII Corps.

the 101st AB Division was caught without its commander, Major General Maxwell D Taylor, who was attending a conference in the United States. The Assistant Divisional Commander, Brigadier General Gerald J Higgins, was also away in England attending the 'wash-up' of Operation MARKET GARDEN. The 'Screaming Eagles' as they were known, were under the command of Brigadier General Anthony C McAuliffe, the Divisional Artillery Commander.

101st Airborne Division.

The 82nd was on the road first, closely followed by the long truck convoys of the 101st. It had been such a rush to get the men on the move that most had neither weapons nor helmets and some were still wearing their summer uniforms fresh from being dragged back off leave. These supply problems would be remedied en-route, or at their destination.

By evening of the 17th General Lauchert's 2nd Panzer Division had found the northern road leading into Clervaux open. A small combined team of infantry and tanks brushed aside the solitary 57mm anti-tank gun guarding the bridge at the railway station. This now left the main body of armour free to roam through the streets unhindered. At 1825 Fuller telephoned Cota to tell him German tanks were directly outside his Command Post in the hotel. With that he and some of his staff made their escape to the west. He was captured later.

In the Chateau at the southern bridge of the town 102 officers

A current photograph of Clervaux Castle taken from the heights of the Marnach Road.

Panthers advancing during the German advance.

and men still held out in the strongly built fortress. These men, were a mixture of the Regimental Headquarters Company, mainly clerks and such like. These men held the bridge for most of the night until the arrival at dawn of the Panther Battalion of the 3rd Panzer Regiment. Rifle fire bounced off the huge Panther tanks as they clanked by on their way to Bastogne. Behind them infantry, supported by self-propelled 88s, battered the chateau into submission and forced the Americans to surrender.

Middleton at VIII Corps headquarters in Bastogne was beginning to get a picture of what was happening, obviously Bastogne would be next on the Germans' list of objectives. He called on his only armored reserve, the Combat Command Reserve (CCR)of the 9th Armored Division. This was made up of the 52nd Armored Infantry Battalion, 2nd Tank Battalion, 9th Armored Engineers and the 73rd Armored Field Artillery Battalion. It's commander Colonel Joseph H Gilbreth had already positioned his Combat Command in the village of Oberwampach, immediately to the rear of the

9th Armored Division

threatened 28th Division's centre, when orders came through from VIII Corps. He was told to form two road blocks on the main road leading from the east into Bastogne. This order came to him at 21.40, ten minutes after word was received that the enemy had crossed the Clerf. The two road blocks were to be on the main road (N12) one near the village of Lullange, at a junction named Antoniushof where the Clervaux road meets the north-south road from St Vith to Bastogne. The other block planned as a backup and was positioned three miles southwest near the village of Allerborn, at a junction called Fe'itsch. Hold at all costs was emphasized to them.

The forces Colonel Gilbreth had available, with the units of the Combat Command Reserve, were far from adequate when faced with the task of stopping an entire panzer division.

Gilbreth split his forces into three, to the Antoniushof road junction he sent Task Force Rose, named after it's commander Captain L K Rose, this consisted of Company A, 2nd Tank Battalion; Company C, 52nd Armored Infantry Battalion and a platoon of 9th Armored Engineers. The roadblock at Fe'itsch, was manned by Task Force Harper (Lieutenant Colonel Ralph S Harper), which was made up of Company C and part of Company D, 2nd Tank Battalion; Company B, 52nd Armored Infantry Battalion and a platoon of Company C, 9th Armored Engineers; five hundred yards behind these last units was Headquarters Company. The third task force was TF Booth (Lieutenant-Colonel Robert M Booth). This group was made up of what was virtually left of CCR to range on the high ground north of the main highway (N12) between the two roadblocks and protect Gilbreth's HQ and the nearby 73rd AFAB and the independent 58th AFAB. Clervaux was only about five miles due east of these positions and was already aflame.

Gilbreth set up his Headquarters in a large house across the road from the church in Longvilly. He had outposts set up around the village in the form of three light tanks, one platoon from C Company 482nd AAA (AW) (Anti Aircraft Artillery Automatic Weapons Battalion) and a few half tracks, clerks, mechanics and cooks also helping in the defences.

Unofficial insignia of the 482 AAA (AW) Battalion.

An excerpt from the 482nd AAA (AW) official history reads:

A picture of Longvilly today, Headqarters Combat Command R.

'Longvilly, at this time, was nothing more than another village to us but little did we know that we would never forget it. Headquarters established a C.P. in town in one of the few houses while the sections went into firing positions around the outskirts. Every round of reserve ammo was distributed to the men for an attack was imminent. Captain Lovoi visited the sections and instructed them to hold their positions at all cost.

US Armored Infantrymen take cover as German shells land behind them.

Shermans of the 10th Armored Division preparing to move out.

We were to hold our present positions until we could bolster our lines with elements of the 10th Armored Division which was on the way to us. There was little to do but wait for the attacking Germans and pray that the 10th Armored would arrive soon. The sections were subjected to intense artillery fire all night long and history was being written.'

In addition to CCR, Middleton had to hand some combat engineers who had been involved in such jobs as road repairs and tree felling. These engineers were told to draw weapons, something they had not had to do for some time. The 158th Engineer Combat Battalion was to form a screen in front of Bastogne and by the early morning of the 18th were digging in on a line stretching between Foy and Neffe.

The 35th Combat Engineer Battalion had been assigned as VIII Corps Headquarters guard, and so could not be released immediately for adding to the screen. Shortly after midnight CCR was in position, further to the east the 110th Infantry

On the outskirts of Mageret this Sherman was stopped by a German 88mm shell and then was finished off by a Panzerfaust.

Regiment was still struggling to hold back the German flood.

At 0830 on 18 December, armored infantrymen on the road facing Clervaux, at the northern roadblock, spotted three German tanks with infantry rolling out of the early morning fog. These were elements of the Reconnaissance Battalion of General Lauchert's 2nd Panzer Division. The armored infantry withdrew to their tank positions and thirty minutes later the tankers also saw the panzers nudging their way towards them. The American tankers chose their moment and then let rip, knocking out one Mk IV and crippling the other two. Only a few minutes later an entire German tank column came into view, coming straight for them from the north. The Shermans opened fire and the lead German tank stopped and turned back.

The 73rd AFAB joined in and put a concentration of shells down into the area of the 2nd Panzer Division. The Germans likewise brought up their own artillery and fired smoke to cover their movements. There was a bit of a lull, whilst the Reconnaissance Battalion felt out the strength of the American road block and awaited the arrival of their heavy Panther tanks. These arrived at about 1100 and at the same time the shelling intensified. Another smoke screen was laid by the Germans which took over an hour to lift and clear. After it did, the Panthers had moved to within 800 yards of the American line and started firing at the helpless Shermans. One flared up and started burning, another's gun was made useless and a third in frantic manoeuvring threw a track.

But they gave as good as they got and managed to knock out three German tanks. More panzers were noticed, this time coming in from the right. Some Shermans rushed over and destroyed one, sending the others scuttling back for cover. The Germans soon realized that the weakest spot was from the north and concentrated their attack from that direction. Task Force Rose was now fighting on three sides against an overwhelming opposition. Task Force Harper was aware of what was happening to their companions up the road but were refused permission to send them aid. Middleton was in total control and would not allow it.

Lieutenant DeRoche, commander of A Company 2nd Tank Battalion, finally received instructions to pull out and attack the Germans now on the road to Bastogne behind them. Task Force Rose managed to limp away, and took up its new positions near the village of Wincrange where it set up another road block. At nightfall the Germans started firing white phosphorus shells into their positions causing the Shermans to 'button up'. The crews could hear the panzers moving all around them, and during the night more orders were received to pull back to the vicinity of Task Force Harper. This they found impossible as the 2nd Panzer Division had control of the entire area, so what was left of Task Force Rose set off across country.

Task Force Harper consolidated their defensive positions and awaited their turn. Orders were received 'Hold at all cost and to

Task Force Rose's road block at Antoniushaft now a roundabout.

A 10th Armored Division Sherman knocked out of action near Bastogne.

the last man. Help is on its way.'

Suddenly, out of the blackness of the night, the attack came – it was 2000 hours. Tigers and Panthers blasted into Harper's positions and with the advantage of their new infra-red night-sights the German tanks ran amok. They machine-gunned the infantry and punched huge holes into the Shermans. All was complete chaos. After four hours of total hell, Harper ordered what small amount of survivors there were to pull out and fight their way back to Longvilly. Some survivors, including Harper himself, worked their way up to the town of Houffalize and tried to set up defensive positions there. It was at Houffalize on the night 18/19 that Colonel Harper, whilst dismounting from his tank, was caught in a hail of machine-gun fire and killed .

Other stragglers from both task forces escaped west to the village of Longvilly where CCR Headquarters was situated.

General Heinrich von Lüttwitz:
'The 2nd Panzer Division was moving fast, It had met heavy resistance in Clervaux from elements of the 28th Infantry

54

Division, but without further contact with the enemy it moved along rapidly to a point on the Longvilly road. At the road crossing immediately east of Allerborn there was a panzer fight lasting about one hour with heavy losses to American Armor. When this engagement terminated, 2nd Panzer Division again moved rapidly on to Bourcy, just east of Noville.'

The US 73rd Armoured Field Artillery Battalion was now in the vicinity of Longvilly, and was pouring shells down onto the two roadblocks. Gilbreth wondered why the Germans had not followed up with an attack on Longvilly. At that particular time General Lauchert's 2nd Panzer Division was more concerned about its primary objective, the Meuse. He had turned his column off the main highway just under a mile outside Longvilly and was bypassing Bastogne to the north. The men in Longvilly breathed a sigh of relief, but the German move trapped Task Force Booth.

Booth had lost radio contact with his headquarters and so during the night he had decided to save his men and move across country to establish a safer position. At the front of the long column there were about eighty men in half-tracks led by Major Eugene A Watts of the 52nd Armored Infantry Battalion. They rolled through the village of Hardingny and moved left. To their front they spotted a number of German personnel carriers. At once, Watts and his men opened fire, using their personal weapons and the machine guns mounted on the half-tracks. They did the enemy some serious damage and were happy with their results. Suddenly all hell broke loose at the rear of the American column, which had just got into Hardingny. It was being shelled and machine-gunned. Vehicles were blowing up everywhere and no matter which way they turned they bumped into Germans, in fact, they had collided into the main force from the 2nd Panzer Division bypassing Bastogne.

For many of the survivors it would take up to six days of careful walking before they finally reached the safety of the Bastogne perimeter. Major Watts broke his group into small units and told them to only travel at night and make their way back to friendly positions. Two days later Watts and his group made contact with the 101st Airborne's out-posts near Foy and was led into Bastogne. These men were fed and Watts went on to brief McAuliffe on the situation regarding the enemy and

The rough track. Bayerlein and his Panzer Lehr passed along from Niederwampagh to Mageret.

Task Force Booth. He was then given command of Team SNAFU (Snafu is an American term which stands for Situation Normal All F——d Up) which comprised of personnel from all the different units that had also managed to reach Bastogne.

With 2nd Panzer Division heading north-west towards the Meuse, Panzer Lehr and 26th VGD were to carry on and seize Bastogne. General Bayerlein's Panzer Lehr had broken free of the terrific traffic jam leading from the Clerf valley. Bayerlein, who was up front with his tanks, decided to split his forces at the village of Eschweiler and utilize the two roads leading to Bastogne. He led his column comprising of a Panzergrenadier Regiment and about fifteen Mk IV tanks up the right-hand road and headed towards the road junction at Fe'itsch. A mile short of it he turned left onto a minor road that leads directly to Bastogne. He could hear and see the fighting going on at the junction, but continued on. At about 1800 the column drew up at the village of Niederwampach only six miles from its goal.

Surely now, he thought, he would win the race for Bastogne. From Niederwampach he had two choices, there was a road leading south which would bring the Germans onto a hard surfaced road that led to their prize, or he could continue on a secondary road which would eventually bring him into the village of Mageret. He decided to take the most direct route, the side road. Belgians in the area (who obviously were none too pleased at having the Germans back again) had told him that the road was excellent. The road soon petered out into little more than a muddy farm track and Bayerlein started having serious reservations. Even so, the force managed to proceed, slipping and sliding until it came into Mageret. Defenders of Mageret, a small detachment belonging to the 158th Engineer Combat Battalion, were no match and Bayerlein soon had control of the village.

Late in the evening gunfire was heard behind CCR positions, this was when the Germans entered Mageret. Colonel Gilbreth decided to get his men out. At about midnight he ordered what was left of CCR and some attached troops from the 28th Division's 110th Regt which had drifted in, to begin a withdrawal via Mageret. The column got so disorganized leaving Longvilly that it blocked the exit to the village. Gilbreth saw what was happening and did not dare order any further movement until daylight. The 73rd AFAB was told to disperse westward, which it did, each battery covering the other. Once in its assigned position it took up firing again at any enemy targets north, south or east of it.

At about the same time as men of the CCR were contemplating their chances of survival, Combat Command B from the 10th Armored Division arrived in Bastogne. It was just before 1600, 18 December. Middleton asked Colonel Roberts, commander of Combat Command B (CCB), how many teams he could make available to man the defensive perimeter that was forming around Bastogne. Roberts replied that he only had sufficient personnel for three effective groups, and promptly split them as follows: Team 'O'Hara' (Lieutenant-Colonel James O'Hara) moved out south-east to occupy an area around Wardin on the Luxembourg road. Team 'Cherry' (Lieutenant Colonel Henry T Cherry) moved out onto the Longvilly road, and finally, Team 'Desobry' (Major William R Desobry) went out onto the Noville road north of Bastogne.

Team Cherry's advance patrols had reached the outskirts of Longvilly during the evening of the 18th and made contact with CCR's command post. CCR had no orders other than to 'hold at all cost', but they were finding it increasingly difficult to do. At this time their southern road-block was still holding.

The advance guard of Team Cherry was commanded by 1st Lieutenant Edward P Hyduke. He had the area reconnoitred and discerned that the main weakness in the eastern defences was just south of Longvilly. Here he stationed his cavalry platoon of four Shermans and seven light Stuart tanks.

At about midnight 18/19th December, Hyduke heard that CCR was going to pull out. He was to be the rear guard in Longvilly, at the same time he also learnt that Mageret had been taken from the scratch force of the 158th Combat Engineers defending it. He surmised that the only way not to get cut-off himself, was to forcibly smash his team through Mageret. Hyduke's force was leaving Mageret for Longvilly using the

The Grotto of St Michael on the outskirts of Longvilly, where Team Cherry and CCR, 9th Armored Division stood firm against overwhelming German forces.

front door. The Germans, at the same time, entered the village through the back door. Colonel Cherry, knowing that Mageret was now in German hands, sent an armoured infantry company under Captain William F. Ryerson to try and open the road through the village.

During the night of 18 December, the German 77th and 78th Infantry Regiments from the 26th VGD had been trying to take Longvilly. Their orders were to pass through that village and head for Bizory, where they were to attack Bastogne from the north and north-east. Fires from the burning houses illuminated numerous targets for the guns of the attackers, but the Americans stubbornly held on until daybreak.

At 08.30, 19 December, during a lull in the fighting, the main body of CCR began to withdraw from Longvilly. As the column of vehicles approached Mageret they found the road blocked by Team Ryerson from CCB, 10th Armored Division. Tanks and lorries piled up behind each other completely trapped. With Lieutenant Hyduke and the rearguard of the CCR fighting a delaying action in Longvilly, and Captain Ryerson's unit trying to recapture Mageret, all was chaos.

An eye-witness account from the 482d AAA (AW) Battalion (SP):

As we waited for an opening into Bastogne, it became very evident that the enemy was gaining fast in his drive, for their artillery began to fall closer and closer to our column, until finally it was hitting in our immediate area. Vehicles and men were hit by flying shrapnel and the screams for medics were drowned by the crack of the bursting artillery shells. Split second decisions had to be made and it was decided to take as much of our equipment across country as we could. Tec 5 E Humphrey and Tec 5 Frank Walsh were injured before we could move, by flames from a gasoline truck which had been set afire by the bursting artillery. Meantime, the crew of an M-16 halftrack distinguished themselves by winning a battle with a Tiger Royal tank. Tec 5 Davidson was the only gunner on the track and he was wounded in the leg. When he saw the approaching tank he

Field Artillery of the 9th Armored Division move into positions.

*asked to be lifted into the machine gun turret. Davidson opened
fire with his four guns but not before his two cannoneers had
been wounded by the machine guns on the tank. PVT Stewts
was hit on the hand and Reinhardt in the leg. As the tank met
the fire of the machine guns, the commander evidently thought
he'd found the whole American army for the tank could not run
fast enough to get away from the continuous rain of slugs. The
M-16 had been put out of action in the engagement so the three
wounded men abandoned it and made their way to an aid
station.*

*When a count was taken in the encircled city, it was found
that we had suffered heavily at the hands of the enemy. Most all
of our personal equipment was lost, over half of our vehicles and
only about fifty able bodied men were left in the entire battery.
We were organized in such a manner that we could do the most
to help in the defence of the city. We had our first hot meal in
days then snatched a few hours of sleep in a hotel before 0400 the
next morning when we were awakened and informed that
regardless of what happened, we were going to hold this vital
road junction.'*

One regiment from the 26th VGD started to advance, within
minutes it came under direct fire from Lieutenant Hyduke's
men occupying the high ground around St Michael's Grotto. It
took several hours before Kokott could get his men organized
for another attack. When they finally did attack they were aided
by a large force loaned from Panzer Lehr.

Bayerlein with his Panzer Lehr Division needed to reduce
Longvilly to open the road. He got together a Panzer Grenadier
Regiment, a tank destroyer battalion and an artillery battalion
for the purpose. When this battle group reached a vantage point
overlooking the road from the south-west, they were amazed to
see, only about a mile away, the whole road jammed with
American vehicles.

About the same time, von Lauchert's 2nd Panzer Division
had been shelled by the 73rd AFAB on the Bourcy road. A
battery of 88s were brought up to return fire from the south-
west of the same road. If this was not enough, the 26th VGD also
brought up a large number of anti-tank guns and artillery from
their positions southeast of Longvilly.

The road south of Longvilly then received perhaps the

Generalleutnant **Bayerlein, Commander of Panzer Lehr Division.**

greatest barrage put down during the battle. It was a fearful
Werfer and artillery attack and the air became thick with red hot
shards of shrapnel. Men in the St Michael's Grotto area
dismounted their vehicular weapons and carried them to the
high ground either side of the road setting them up in ground
positions. The column had nowhere to go, tanks and half-tracks
exploded everywhere.

However, the American tankers had conducted themselves
so well that at one point von Lauchert thought that he was being
counter-attacked by a large force. At least eight of his Panzers
had been reduced to flaming wrecks. The encounter had also
taken its toll on the American tankers and by early afternoon all
that remained of Lieutenant Hyduke's tank force were a couple
of light Stuart tanks. These could not manoeuvre without
bringing down a hail of fire and eventually the crews had little
choice but to render them useless and abandon them.

The armoured infantry left their half-tracks and, along with

Tank Destroyers from the 705th TD Battalion in positions between houses.

the tankers, headed west for what they thought would be safety. The main bulk of Team Cherry under Captain William F Ryerson had been ordered by Lieutenant-Colonel Cherry to withdraw westwards. This was no easy matter with all the clutter lining the road to Mageret. The leading Sherman was only a few hundred yards outside the village when it received a direct hit and brewed up. The road was now completely blocked and any thought of a headlong drive through the village of Mageret was now out of the question. They could not move anywhere without drawing fire from Panzer Lehr's guns or the guns of 26th VGD Reconnaissance Battalion, which now held Mageret. All Ryerson could do was to cling on to what little bit of the village they had. He sent a message to Cherry:

> *'Having tough time, Enemy shooting flares and knocking out our vehicles with direct fire.'*

As the main part of Team Cherry was fighting between

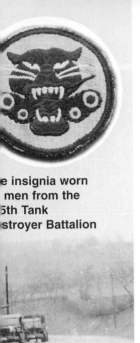

Longvilly and Mageret, Colonel Cherry and his headquarters troops were having a tough time of their own. He had made his headquarters in a large stone chateau a few hundred yards south of the crossroads at Neffe. The American outposts were hit by a detachment of panzers and supporting infantry. The GIs managed to hit one tank with a bazooka but were in danger of being overwhelmed and fell back to the chateau.

The men of the US 3rd Tank Battalion's command post (Team Cherry) held the Germans at bay for four hours, meeting every rush with a hail of bullets from automatic weapons taken from their vehicles and emplaced behind the thick stone walls. In the end a few Germans managed to get close enough to throw incendiary grenades through the windows of the chateau. In no time the place was ablaze. Fortunately for them reinforcements came out from Bastogne to help them withdraw. Under covering fire, Cherry and his men pulled out and headed for the next village west, Mont. At the same time he sent a message to CCB Commander,

'We are pulling out. We're not driven out but burned out.'

Through the rest of that day the force fighting at Mageret waited for reinforcements to arrive to help them break out, but nothing

The Heintz Barracks in Bastogne. In December 1944 it was Middleton's and then McAuliffe's headquarters.

happened. As midnight came around a radio message came through from CCB telling Ryerson to withdraw north-west to Bizory. At daybreak Ryerson took what was left of his men and vehicles, and forty minutes later slowly and painfully entered the American lines at Bizory.

General Heinrich von Lüttwitz:

During the night, Panzer Lehr Division got on a country road to Mageret. The point of the Division got to Neffe early in the morning and reduced the road block. When Panzer Lehr Division came to a halt in front of the Chateau Neffe, a regiment was ordered to go immediately from Bizory to Bastogne. It thus was deployed in a manner which put its line directly against the deployed American infantry lines. When this combat team was stopped in the north, another combat team from Panzer Lehr Division was sent southward against Wardin and Marvie with the mission of getting to Bastogne. This combat team was brought to a stop about one-half Kilometre southeast of Marvie. From this time on we were stopped on this line.'

Over a quarter of the CCB had been lost during 19 December, which totalled 175 Officers and men. Not to mention vehicle losses, which came to seventeen half-tracks, and about the same number of tanks. Casualties in CCR were even greater, in-fact, it almost ceased to exist anymore. There seems no doubt that these two forces, CCR and Task Force Cherry had been sacrificed in order to slow the Germans up. But slow them up they certainly did.

Colonel Eugene A.Watts said:

'As a Major I took over command of the 52nd Armored Infantry Battalion (part of CCR of 9th Armd Division) on 17 December 1944, and remained commander until the following February 1945. CCR was located directly to the rear of the 106th Infantry Division and the 28th Infantry Division as part of General Middleton's Corps. After the German breakthrough on 16 December, the Corps Commander (in essence) sacrificed CCR in order to save time to get the 101st Airborne Division and part of 10th Armored Division into Bastogne. We were ordered to set up road-blocks at several places to slow down its panzers and other leading German units. These road blocks were doomed to failure because we were ordered to use only one company of Armored Infantry and one company of tanks at each road block.

We fought hard but could not stop a German Panzer Division, although we did slow them down. The commanders of our Tank Battalions, and several Company Commanders and about ten platoon leaders were killed or wounded at these road blocks. We retreated towards Bastogne and by 20 December about 210 men and officers of my 52nd Armored Infantry Battalion finally arrived in the vicinity of Bastogne. We lost more than 700 killed wounded or captured in about three or four days. We were first placed under the command of 325th Glider Infantry Regiment (of 101st Airborne) for four days, then later under command of a Combat Command of the 10th Armored Division. They supplemented my 52nd Armored Infantry Battalion with about 250 SNAFU [men without an assigned unit] soldiers with our primary mission to protect the artillery battalions near the Senonchamps area.

Although General Middleton was commended by General Eisenhower and General Bradley for successfully slowing down the Germans to get 101st Airborne Division into Bastogne, CCR did not appreciate being sacrificed to accomplish this. I lost my jeep with all of my clothes, camera etc, and walked into Bastogne.'

Shermans from the 9th Armored Division awaiting fuel and orders to move out.

Armored infantry half-tracks crossing a pontoon bridge head for Bastogne.

General Heinrich von Lüttwitz:

'The point of 2 Panzer Division was at Noville, with the remaining elements of the Division strung out along the road through Bourcy and back to the northwest of Allerborn. At this time, the Corps Commander got word that strong American armoured forces were moving from Bourcy to Longvilly and, therefore, were threatening his flank. The forward elements of 26 Volks Gren Div were at this moment on Hill 499 southwest of

Longvilly. The 2 Panzer Division brought up its anti tank battalion and stationed it so as to block the road. At the same time, the anti tank battalion of Pz Lehr Div was pushed through 26 Volks Gren Div, which took up positions on Hill 499. Also, at the same time, all of the artillery of 26 Volks Gren Div was ordered to fire on the area west of Longvilly, where the American armor had become entangled.'

During the 18/19 December, General Lüttwitz had expected word at anytime to say that Bastogne had fallen, but none was forthcoming. The Americans had pipped the Germans to the post, although it was a close run race. For now reinforcements were arriving in the shape of the 101st Airborne Division.

The Airborne Division had en-trucked and made the journey south in good time. The drive was mostly in darkness, in pouring rain and brief snow flurries. After a bit of a mix up the 82nd Airborne were sent to Werbomont to shore-up the northern sector, and the 101st carried on to Bastogne. The 107 miles trip was made in eight hours and the leading column arrived in its assembly area around Mande St Etienne just west of Bastogne by midnight. By 0900 on 19 December, all four regiments of the 101st had arrived and General McAuliffe started his preparations.

The division consisted of the 501st Parachute Infantry Regiment (PIR) (Lieutenant Colonel Julian J Ewell), the 506th PIR (Colonel Robert F Sink), 502nd PIR (Lieutenant Colonel Steve A Chappuis) and the 327th Glider Infantry Regiment (GIR) (Colonel Joseph H Harper), attached to the 327th was the 1st Battalion 401st GIR.

Also arriving in Bastogne at about the same time was the 705th Tank Destroyer Battalion, sent down from the Ninth Army up north. This battalion was equipped with M18 Hellcats armed with the new 76mm long barrelled gun, which put it on equal terms with the German Tigers with their 88mm guns. The 755th Field Artillery Battalion with its 155mm howitzers had received orders to leave its original position and head for Bastogne. By chance the 969th FAB had been supporting the 28th Division with its medium howitzers when it found itself within the Bastogne perimeter. The field artillery battalions were sent south-west, to the Villeroux and Senonchamps area. The 420th Armored Field Artillery Battalion, CCB 10th Armored Division was already in place. From these positions all the FABs would be able to lay down fire anywhere in the area when required.

Floyd Foster, serving with the 420th Armored Field Artillery Battalion, 10th Armored Division recalls:

The 10th Armored Division withdrew from the front in the Saar River area, and proceeded northward as fast as possible to shore up the defences of the First Army north of Luxembourg City in Belgium, and the sector in Luxembourg itself. Having travelled all night, CCB arrived in Bastogne on the 18th. The 420th AFA Bn, had loaded up on gasoline and ammunition at Luxembourg City, with all we could carry with us... and left our supply trains there, to get additional big shells for our M-7's [105mm Howitzers on an open tank chassis] *and more gasoline and small arms ammo. They were to rejoin us as soon as possible.'*

Technician 4th Grade Floyd Foster, 420th Armored Field Artillery Batalion 10th Armored Division

By 20 December, the 420th AFA Bn had positioned itself west of Bastogne proper, with the fire direction post and battalion headquarters set up at Senonchamps, (approximately three kilometres west on the Marche road). From this position we proceeded to support our three teams of 10th Armored tanks and infantry... Team O'Hara (south of Wardin, on the Wiltz road – south-east)...Team Cherry (At Longvilly to the east)...and Team Desobry (north at Noville).

Our 105s had a range of approximately seven miles (12,300 yards) and we were able to complete fire missions for all the teams from our location.'

Within two hours of its arrival the 705th Tank Destroyer Battalion had all its elements occupying defensive positions along the line.

Lieutenant Wayne E. Tennant (705th TD Battalion):

'The 705th TD Bn arrived in the Bastogne area on the 18 December 1944, with orders to report to the 101st Airborne Division. I was a Company Commander of Company C and my orders were to report to and support a 101st Airborne Infantry unit in a grove of trees [On the road to Foy] *about three miles north of Bastogne. I left my Headquarters platoon and one platoon of tank destroyers in Bastogne and took two platoons of tank destroyers (eight TDs) with me. I found the grove of trees in the dark, near midnight, kept one*

Lieutenant Wayne E. Tennant 705th TD Battalion.

platoon there with me and sent the other platoon on into Foy.
The next morning just as it was nearing daylight we started
receiving heavy fire. We also started receiving casualties, and I
was one of them'.

Middleton, who we have already seen had his headquarters in
the old army barracks in Bastogne, was advised to shift his
command southwest to the town of Neufchateau. This he did,
but he remained in order to brief McAuliffe on the disposition
of his make-shift defence.

The 1st Battalion of the 501st were to set out immediately to
reinforce CCR and Task Force Cherry. McAuliffe told the
commander, Colonel Ewell:

'Move out along this road to the east at 1800, make contact
with the enemy, attack and clear up the situation.'

The 1st Battalion got no further than the village of Neffe.
However, it was able to help Cherry and his staff escape the
inferno of his command post at the chateau. In a classic three
battalion attack the paratroopers pushed elements of the Panzer
Lehr out of Bizory to the north of Mageret and held firm.

Colonel Roberts of the 10th Armored Division had put his
arm around the young 26 year old Major Desobry in a fatherly
gesture and told him,

'By tomorrow morning you'll probably be nervous. Then
you'll probably want to pull out. When you begin thinking like
that, remember I told you NOT to pull out.'

Desobry spent a sleepless night in the village of Noville; with
the morning came erratic attacks from German tanks. It was
difficult to see anything, as the early morning fog was thickest
in this particular area. At about mid morning the pea soup fog
suddenly lifted. The American defenders were amazed to see
the whole area crawling with German armour. The 2nd Panzer
Division, on its way north-west towards the Meuse, had hit
Noville. Desobry's tank gunners started firing with everything
they had. The enemy had been caught by surprise and their
vehicles made excellent targets. To the north could be seen
fourteen German tanks racing in column along a high ridge. It
was like a shooting gallery, the small force of tank destroyers
with their 90mm guns picked off ten of them in quick
succession.

It was not long before ammunition was running short so

Desobry radioed Colonel Roberts at CCB Headquarters to ask permission to pull back a couple of miles to regroup. Roberts replied, 'You can use your own judgement about withdrawing. But I'm sending a battalion of paratroopers to reinforce you.' 'I'll get ready to counterattack,' replied Desobry. It was just the sort of thing that headquarters in Bastogne wanted to hear.

Team O'Hara, situated to the southeast of Wardin, had seen very little action, so far things had been quiet in the sector when elsewhere the sound of battle kept flaring up. This was worrying O'Hara – was something unpleasant gathering in the fog which shrouded the area? He called one of his officers over, Lieutenant John Drew Devereaux, and told him to take a Jeep and patrol north to the village of Wardin. All was quiet there, so Devereaux, with his two companion, drove on eastwards. The fog began lifting and visibility started to improve all round. Suddenly they spotted, in the near distance, German half-tracks heading their way. Lieutenant Devereaux was at the wheel and responding to the involuntary cry of 'Krauts!' he spun the Jeep around and, flattening the accelerator to the floor, raced back to report to O'Hara.

They had bumped into a reconnaissance patrol belonging to Panzer Lehr. At that precise moment a large part of Bayerlein's armour was heading northeast to eradicate, what he considered to be, the peril behind him. He still thought that there was a large American presence at Longvilly.

Major General William H Morris (Centre), Commander of the 10th Armored Division, confers with Lieutenant General Patton.

U.S. Infantry digging in. The conditions were awful.

That same day in Verdun, Eisenhower chaired a conference. The air of which was one of gloom and doom. He began the proceedings by saying,

'The present situation is to be regarded as one of opportunity for us and not of disaster. There will only be cheerful faces at this conference table.'

General Patton was the first to reply. In his normal flamboyant way he blurted out.

'Let's have the guts to let the sons of bitches go all the way to Paris. Then we'll really cut 'em off and chew 'em up.'

Immediately the atmosphere changed; a light-hearted mood descended over the conference. Eisenhower stated that the German attack must not go further than the River Meuse, and Patton he told to make an attack north to help relieve the presure on the struggling US First Army.

'I want you to go to Luxembourg and take charge. When can you start up there.'

'Now,!' answered Patton.

'You mean today.' said Eisenhower. *'I mean as soon as*

72

you've finished with us here.' replied Patton.

Everybody at the table thought Patton was doing his usual thing, of boasting and Eisenhower got annoyed. Patton stood up, lit a cigar and pointed to the bulge on the operations map.

'This time the Kraut has stuck his head in a meat grinder. And this time I've got hold of the handle.'

'All right, George,' said Eisenhower. *'Start your attack no earlier than the twenty-second and no later than the twenty-third.'*

With the meeting finished Patton telephoned his headquarters in Nancy, and told them of his plan. Within a few minutes of the receiver being replaced Patton's Third Army started to wheel the ninety degrees necessary to get them on the new track heading north.

Meanwhile at Bastogne, men were streaming in from all kinds of dissimilar units. The fleeing stragglers were immediately fed, for most had not slept or eaten for two days, before being rearmed and introduced into the defensive ring around the town.

At Noville the 1st Battalion of Colonel Robert F Sink's 506th Parachute Infantry Regiment arrived to aid Team Desobry. The paratroopers commanded by Colonel La Prade linked up with the tanks and La Prade took charge. Within minutes the command post was hit by an artillery shell and La Prade lay dead and Desobry was evacuated badly wounded. The paratroopers, now under command of Major Harwick, had battled against a battalion-size force and along with Team Desobry, now renamed Team Hustead, dug in.

All night the men endured heavy shelling which steadily demolished the village. At dawn two German tanks came crashing into the village, both were destroyed, one by a bazooka, the other by a shell from a Sherman. This was just the start, for by mid-morning the 2nd Panzer Division was throwing everything at Noville and American casualties were mounting by the minute.

At midday, orders were received to fall back on the village of Foy. Men were crowded onto the surviving five Shermans and into the remaining half-tracks and, under cover of a now descending fog, headed south. Just outside Foy the lead half-track stopped. Due to the poor visibility the second half-track in

Glider troops moving out to their positions.

the line ran into the back of the stationary vehicle, effectively blocking the road. At the same time some Germans, who had infiltrated behind the village of Noville, began firing at the stalled convoy. A concentrated fusillade of machine gun and rifle fire put paid to the intruders. Shortly after the column got going it was fired on again, this time by a group of German tanks. Two Shermans were hit, one broke down, and another one got away but was destroyed as it reached Foy. The remaining Sherman was driverless after he had climbed down from his tank to try and sort out the traffic jam and was hit. No other driver could be found, so a group of paratroopers got in it and managed to lead what was left of the defenders of Noville, back to the relative safety of Foy.

General Heinrich von Lüttwitz:

The orders called for 2nd Panzer Division to take Noville under any circumstances, as fast as possible, and it was the troops of that division which carried the attack throughout. The attacks of the two divisions had not been coordinated. Although each division was supposed to proceed within its divisional zone and the faster it moved the better, they were in radio communication at all times, and each division knew what the other was doing. In this phase of the attack they could not change the plan. Before they attacked it was pretty clear that Bastogne would be difficult to take. On 12 December 1944, the Corps Commander issued this order to his division, "Bastogne must be taken eventually from the rear. If it is not taken, it will always remain an ulcer on our lines of communication, and for this reason it will contain too many forces. Therefore, first clear out the whole of Bastogne and then march on." The northernmost infantry regiment of 26 Volks Gren Div had orders after going through Longvilly to proceed through Foy toward Longchamps, and it was elements of this division engaged in this movement which got into 506 PIR rear at Foy and threatened to split 506 and 501 PIR.'

[This was the force that made the split by attacking down the railway towards Bastogne 21 December.]

The commander of the 2nd Panzer Division radioed headquarters for permission to attack south towards Bastogne, but was abruptly told to keep going for the Meuse and forget Bastogne. The task of subduing the town would be for the Panzer Lehr and 26th VGD. The Germans by this time were flowing north and south of Bastogne, clearly probing to find a weak spot in the now forming perimeter defence. They desperately needed to capture Bastogne.

By 20 December, McAuliffe had all his reinforcements in and around Bastogne. To the east, still holding, was Team Cherry along with the 501st Parachute Infantry Regiment; to the north-east at Foy was the 506th Parachute Infantry Regiment; the northern perimeter was being held by the 502nd Parachute Infantry Regiment (PIR). Finally, the southern area was being covered by the 327th Glider Infantry Regiment (GIR). Scattered amongst these regiments was aid in the form of Robert's CCB 10th Armored Division and the 705th Tank Destroyer Battalion. The artillery was well within the comparative safety of the perimeter and could lay a barage down anywhere around it when called upon to do so.

The line was tested twice that day. Elements of Panzer Lehr attacked from the southeast, hitting Team O'Hara, manning a road block near the village of Marvie. Tanks and armoured personnel carriers crashed through the block and entered the village itself. Glider troops from Colonel Harper's 327 GIR were rushed over to give aid to the hard-pressed tankers and house to house fighting ensued. After about two hours the Germans had been routed and Marvie was firmly in American hands once again.

Meanwhile, German infantry supported by tanks and self-propelled artillery, hit the left-hand side of Ewell's 501st PIR near the village of Bizory. After a hard fight and minus several tanks hit by anti-tank fire from the American lines the Germans sought cover. It was now that the artillery was called on for the first time. A twenty-minute concentration landed on the hapless Germans killing and wounding many.

Although the *Volksgrenadiers* lost many men they continued their attack that evening. After an artillery barrage, panzers and infantry attacked through Neffe towards Bastogne. The American artillery opened up once more creating a wall of fire. Infantry that succeeded in surviving this were promptly cut down by machine-gun fire from Ewell's 1st Battalion. In unison with this attack another regiment of *Volksgrenadiers* attacked Ewell's southern or right-hand line. As darkness fell the American infantry could hear the Germans moving about, and laid down fire in their direction. Screams and yells could be heard as bullets found targets. Next morning's light revealed the grim sight of rows of dead Germans hanging on barbed wire. In the darkness the Germans had got themselves entangled amongst some farmers' wire fences which crossed the fields in front of the American positions.

With a lull in the fighting on 20 December, McAuliffe decided to go to Neufchateau and see Middleton; he wanted to reassess the situation. McAuliffe told the Corps commander that he could hold out for perhaps another two days. Middleton was pleased and said:

'Good luck Tony, Now don't get yourself surrounded.'

McAuliffe returned in his jeep to Bastogne, no sooner had he entered the safety of the perimeter than the Germans moving north and south of the town cut the Neufchateau road, effectively encircling the town.

CHAPTER FOUR

ENCIRCLEMENT

During the night 19/20 December the 2nd Panzer Division, moving north of Bastogne, captured the town of Ortheuville where the main road headed north-west to Marche. This effectively sealed in the defenders of Bastogne from the north.

General Heinrich von Lüttwitz:

'The 2nd Panzer Division, after attacking and taking Noville at about 1500, 20 December 1944, moved its reconnaissance elements on westward as far as Salle, north of Flamierge. They then drew fire from a road block directly to the west. These reconnaissance forces then turned northwest of the road block. At 2400, the reconnaissance team reached the bridge by Ortheuville. We then proceeded to build up the bridgehead in front of Tenneville.

THE GERMAN ATTACK ON BASTOGNE

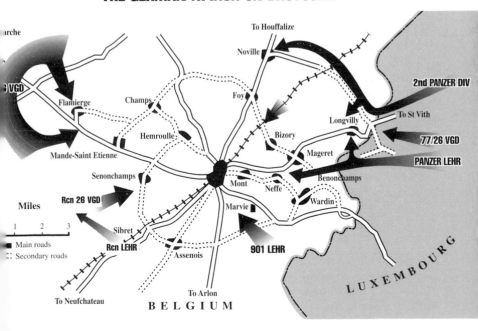

'We had assumed from the beginning that the US 101 Airborne Division would remain in Bastogne and fight. Having been given their zones, we assumed that both divisions could proceed in good style, and could keep together without too much difficulty. When we found that 2nd Panzer Division could not continue its advance westward past Tenneville, I proposed to the Army Commander [Generalleutnant Manteuffel] that we change the plan and concentrate all our effort against Bastogne, using all our forces to take the town. This was disapproved; instead, we were ordered to continue in the general line of advance given in the first order, with Panzer Lehr Division advancing south of Bastogne and 2nd Panzer Division advancing north of Bastogne. As they advanced, 26 Volksgrenadier Division was to close in behind, invest the town from the east, and subsequently take Bastogne when the occasion became favourable.'

Panzer Lehr cut across the south face of Bastogne. The Germans were changing their tactics. Lüttwitz was becoming displeased about the state of his troops as they tried to hammer their way into Bastogne from the east. He was aware that American reinforcements had arrived and that the whole side of the town had now been strengthened. His troops had probed and probed but had found no way in from that direction. Also, his Panzer Lehr and 26th VGD were gathering strength by the hour, as more and more of its elements began catching up. One of these, the 39th Regiment of the 26th VGD, was immediately behind the attacking Corps. Lüttwitz decided to tell Bayerlein to leave one unit, the 901st Panzer Grenadier Regiment, to help out the foot elements of the 26th VGD, with attacks from the east in the area of Neffe. It was put into the line facing Team O'Hara and the 2nd Battalion 327 GIR at Marvie.

Meanwhile, the main bulk of Panzer Lehr was to cut across the south face of the defence perimeter to St Hubert, passing through Hompre and Sibret as it went. At the same time the 26th VGD would move into an assembly point at Remonfosse, a village on the main Bastogne-Arlon road, with a view to attacking Bastogne from the south. So, by the morning of 21 December, German troops were in complete control of all the roads leading into Bastogne.

The war diary of the 327th GIR records, 'It was on this day 20 December, that all roads were cut by the enemy and we were

Private Marcel Lerner, 10th Armored Division chats to a Belgian policeman during a lull in the fighting in Bastogne.

completely surrounded.'

An exerpt from the history of the 705th Tank Destroyer Battalion reads:

> *'That night when Corps called by radio-telephone to ask the situation, the 101st Airborne Division G-3 replied: "Visualise the hole in the doughnut, that's us."'*

Everyone was excited about the American hole in the doughnut – everyone except the forces encircled there. The typical feeling of the men in Bastogne upon learning that they were encircled was clearly expressed by one of the fellows who said, 'The poor bastards, they've got us surrounded.'

That night, Lieutenant-Colonel Clifford Templeton lay in his bedroll, smoking his pipe, his steel helmet clamped on his head as a protection against falling plaster, listening to the shells whistling in and exploding. He turned to the Battalion Supply Sergeant and looked at him thoughtfully. 'Sergeant Byrum,' he said, 'You need a haircut'. Roy K.Byrum, who had been with the Battalion ever since it had been formed, grinned, and asked: 'What do you intend to do, Colonel? Gig me?' The Colonel frowned. 'Sergeant,' he said grimly, 'you are hereby restricted to the area for one week'.

The weather, still very foggy, began to get colder and snow started to fall. This meant that the German tanks that had previously been confined to roads, due to the boggy ground conditions, would now be able to range across country.

Also, on 20 December, Middleton gave McAuliffe complete command of all forces within the perimeter. Up until then McAuliffe and Colonel Roberts of CCB had worked together on an equal footing.

The Americans took stock:

The 101st Airborne was lacking in all sorts of equipment and ammunition due to their hasty move; fortunately CCB was not lacking in anything, and so were in a position to pass needed materiale on to the paratroopers. A huge dump of flour had been found which had been abandoned by the American Red Cross, and so pancakes were to become the staple diet of the defenders. Medical supplies were a cause for concern. During the night of 19/20 December, a German raiding party had overrun the 101st AB Service area around Mande St Etienne capturing most of the medical supplies and few personnel managed to escape. This meant that adequate care for the growing number of wounded could not be guaranteed.

Through most of 21 December the Germans attacked in force, mainly from the north-east, east and south-east. The main threat came when a large force from Kokott's 26th VGD attacked down the Bourcy-Bastogne railway track. This particular spot marked the boundary between the defending 506th and 501st PIR. Although the attack was beaten off, men from the 26th VGD's 77th and 78th Regiments had infiltrated through the boundary gap. A patrol from the 506th discovered the breech and Companies D and F attacked, plugging the hole. Colonel Sink sent his depleted 1st Battalion to rid the area of the infiltrating Germans. During the afternoon things began to quieten down as the *Volksgrenadiers* from the 77th and 78th Regiments tried to sort themselves out.

Prior to Eisenhower's conference, Patton had seen the need to assist the forces resisting the German breakthrough and had released the 4th Armored Division ordering it to head north and join Middleton's VIII Corps.

During the night of 19 December the Combat Command B (CCB) of the 4th Armored Division rolled into its assigned bivouac area near the town of Vaux-les-Rosieres.The following morning General Dager, commanding the CCB, ordered a task force to enter Bastogne. The force consisted of Company A, 8th Tank Battalion, Company C, 10th Armored Infantry Battalion and C Battery 22nd Armored Field Artillery Battalion. Captain Bert P Ezell was placed in command. The mission of Task Force Ezell, as it was designated, was to report to the commander at Bastogne, McAuliffe, learn of the situation, receive instructions and render support if so ordered.

The task force moved up the Neufchateau-Bastogne road and

Armored artillerymen, man their self propelled 105mm Howitzer.

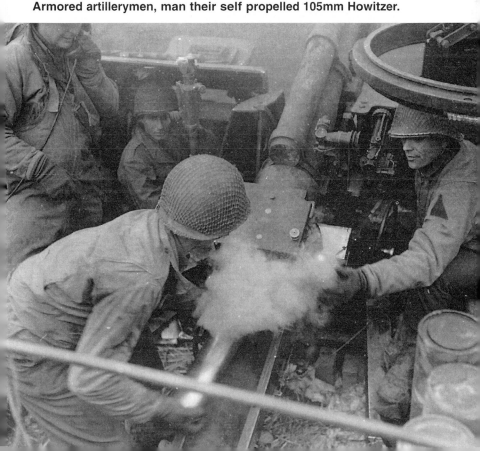

reached the beleaguered town unhindered, without seeing any enemy troops. Once there, Ezell was told to report to Roberts and not McAuliffe. Roberts was in the process of deploying Task Force Ezell when a radio message came through from 4th Armored Division ordering Ezell to bring the Task Force back. Ezell was puzzled by the change of mind but informed Colonel Roberts that he had his orders, and by noon was back on the road again. On the journey back they encountered a GMC truck in a ditch by the side of the road. The truck looked in good shape and the driver was still sitting behind the wheel. But on closer inspection the man was

The insignia of the 4th Armored Division.

A road block manned by two GI's of the 9th Armored Division check the identification cards of a Belgian civilian.

dead, with the top half of his head missing. A bit further on, large wide tank tracks were noticed crossing the road, which they surmised must have been made by a Tiger or Panther. Still further, and they came across the guns and vehicles of about two battalions of artillery abandoned beside the road. It didn't take the men of Task Force Ezell long to work out that a large German force must have cut the road, probably whilst they were in Bastogne. They hitched up as much of the artillery as they could and proceeded post-haste on to the bivouac area of CCB 4th Armored Division encountering no more strange sights. CCB 4th Armored Division were ordered to proceed to Leglise, south-east of Neufchateau, in preparation for a counter-attack that was to be launched the next day (22 December).

It had been Major Kunkel and his *Kampfgruppe* (the Reconnaissance Battalion from the 26th VGD) that had cut the Neufchateau-Bastogne road, opening the way for Panzer Lehr and 26th VGD to get into position for their attack from the west and southwest. The villages they were passing through, south of Bastogne, were virtually undefended and the Germans were growing in confidence that Bastogne would fall.

Seeing all this movement, McAuliffe sent two battalions from the 327th Glider Infantry Regiment to back up the small force made up of the 326th Airborne Engineer Battalion manning road blocks on the roads leading south out of the town.

Heavy fighting now broke out in the south-west as *Kampfgruppe* Kunkel moved out from Sibret towards the village of Villeroux. In that particular area there were the American heavy field artillery battalions, with little more to protect them than a few infantrymen and fourteen tanks from the newly formed Task Force Pyle. Captain H Pyle was the commanding officer of Company C, 2nd Tank Battalion from CCR, 9th Armored Division. Pyle's initial mission was to make hit and run attacks against the enemy, an enemy of whose strength he knew nothing. Kunkel's objectives were the artillery positions.

The Germans made three successive attacks from the direction of Sibret, and were repulsed each time with the aid of the 420th AFA at Senonchamps. Colonel Gilbreth poached a command half-track from the 10th Armored Division and joined his force in Villeroux. At about mid-day the village was hit by heavy mortar and artillery fire and Gilbreth was wounded when a mortar hit his half-track.

Loading TNT charges into the bases of 105mm shells. Men of the 10th Armored Division prepare for action.

Pyle's tanks engaged the panzers but they were forced back to the village of Senonchamps. At least it had bought precious time for the Corps artillery (755th and 969th) to hitch up their 155mm howitzers and follow them to safer positions. Once there, TF Pyle made a stand and, along with help from half-tracks mounting multiple .50 machine guns, blasted away at the Germans. Kunkel suffered so many losses that he was forced to call off the attack for the night.

Team SNAFU, under Major Eugene A. Watts, had been called on to do a house by house search of Bastogne, to find hidden enemy artillery observers, so accurate was the German artillery fire. However, on the morning of 22 December, with Kunkel renewing his attack on Senonchamps, Major Watts was ordered to reinforce Task Force Pyle. In compliance with this directive

A half-track of the 10th A.D. fires on approaching Germans.

TF SNAFU moved out, along with a company from the 327th GIR to help face the new threat coming from the south and south-west.

Artillery rounds were now in short supply. McAuliffe had requested an air-drop of vital and important supplies, but nothing was forthcoming due to the weather conditions. He therefore rationed the guns to ten rounds per day. This decline in American fire-power permitted the Germans to move so freely both north and south.

Floyd Foster, 420th AFAB CCB, 10th Armored Division recalls the feelings of the gunners as stocks of shells dwindled:

Technician 4th Grade Floyd Foster 420th AFAB, 10th Armored Division, (left of picture).

'*Unfortunately our supply trains* [convoys] *had been held up by what appeared to be a German roadblock, and the promised air drop of ammo and gas had been delayed due to poor weather. At the rate we were firing support cover for all these teams, our ammo supplies were getting dangerous low, and by 21 December Headquarters of CCB decided that we should try to send a task force out to break through the roadblock and bring in the trains, particularly for the 420th Artillery. The 420th was to supply at least one half-track that would maintain communications with both the supply trains and battalion headquarters, plus another half-track and a Sherman tank if possible. Two light tanks were assigned from another unit.*

'*At about 11 o'clock on the night of 21 December 1944, Captain John A. McCloskey, our Battalion Assistant S-3, was picked as our vehicle commander, and I was chosen as the radio operator for his command half-track, which was to head this task force. PFC Alfred Grant was our machine-gunner, and Roy Eads may have been our driver, I'm not sure. (Roy was killed in action, possible during this operation). The crew was made up of various personnel who became available for one reason or another. I was 'picked' because we had two operators on our radio, and I could be spared for a short time for this mission.*

'1st Sergeant Wilton Stevens found me, and informed me that I had been chosen to be the radio operator for this mission. I was called to the Operations Room in a schoolhouse, being used as our fire direction center. My officer, Captain Gilbert Oleson, the S-2 of the battalion, filled me in on what was to take place. He had a large-scale map on the wall and he showed me in detail where we hoped to go, and where we currently were. He reminded me that along the road at our headquarters position was a long line of high tension electric line towers extending generally east-west, that were visible above the trees, houses, and snow. He noted the compass direction both outward, and back inward to our position. I took it all in, and I thanked him for spending the time with me. Looking back at it some months later, I realized how naïve I was at the time... and I really didn't know just what Captain Oleson was doing for me... Possibly he actually saved my life or at least my capture.

'Finally, we were ready to take off. Our column consisted of two light tanks at the front, the two half-tracks in the middle, and the Sherman tank in the rear. We had slowly moved along to the south towards Assenois for about five kilometers in the dark, moonless night (no lights were used by any of our vehicles). The noise of our own vehicles echoed in the quiet of the snow-covered landscape. We had just crossed a bridge over a relatively small river...when the noise of the gasoline engines from our own tanks and half-tracks was joined by a low grumble of heavy diesel engines behind us. Unfortunately, diesel engines meant German vehicles, at least armored half-tracks and probably Tiger tanks.

'Suddenly the beautiful dark night that helped hide us was ablaze with lights. The vehicles behind us had turned on their headlights and even some spotlights...White parachute flares were fired as well... and boy did we stand out there on that road! An incendiary shell ignited a barn on the roadside, and things started to get busy... In front of us was a German road block...so we were in rather a tight predicament. Machine guns and small arms fire were joined with some bigger stuff from the German tanks, our two tanks were light tanks with only a 37mm gun on

the turret, so we didn't have much fire power. It seems that our Sherman tank, manned by our maintenance crew, had developed trouble and had to turn back earlier, leaving our half-track as the last vehicle in the column. We found that the entire column was trapped on the road with a limited field of fire, particularly to the rear. We dismounted, took defensive positions, and started firing.

'To the immediate right of the portion of the road, where we deployed, was a fair size hill. I was afraid that the Germans would circle around us and advance on our flank down this hill... Since I was a sergeant at the time, I took Grant with me, and we started up the hill with our carbines as fire power. We yelled our intentions to Captain McCloskey over the roar of gunfire, and proceeded to make our way. About half way up the hill automatic gunfire started to track us.

'Whether it was our own boys, who thought we were Germans, or it was the Germans shooting...we were under severe fire. In the snow going up the hill we were getting out of breath. We fortunately found a drainage ditch about three feet deep, with one foot of water. We 'bellied' into the ditch, caught our breath, and tried to check out where the troops were. The firing stopped tracking us and we could hear some troops coming over the top of the hill..this was bad because all our buddies were below us.

'Grant and I snaked our way in the ditch until we heard the Germans coming down the hill. We lay in the water and tried to camouflage ourselves as best we could. We stayed absolutely still and the Germans passed right by us. All of a sudden we were outside the closing ring. We crawled along the ditch until we were on the right side of the hill, and then moved on up to the top. Here we took a break and evaluated our potential as a fighting force. We had two carbines, and now only two extra clips of ammo remaining, between the two of us. We noted the sizable number of Germans involved, and we finally decided that we would be wise to make our way back to our unit. The only problem was that our task force was beginning to deploy, and I didn't know exactly what they were going to do, nor where they were headed... but one thing I did know and that was where we had come from. We finally decided to work our way back to Headquarters Battery at Senonchamps. I looked at my watch as it started to rain and found that it was almost five o'clock in the morning... (Time sure flies when you're having fun)...We took off

This Sherman tank from the 10th A.D. was captured and used by the Germans early in the fighting, only to be knocked out later by American Bazookas.

our overshoes and our overcoats. *The overcoats were soaking wet from the water in the ditch and weighed a ton. The overshoes seemed too clumsy for the footwork we anticipated. Orienting ourselves we started to infiltrate back through enemy territory.*

'As wet as it was, the rain was a godsend, because it kept the visibility down and held off dawn longer, as well as covering up some of our noise. I had the general direction in mind, but we couldn't go back the way we came (on the road) because the enemy had blocked if off.

'To begin with, I knew we had to cross back over the river, and it took us about two hours to find a safe and shallow place to wade it. We finally found a place that was about waist deep and crossed. Boy... was that water cold. We avoided all the little hamlets and roads, and any signs of people just to be safe. This meant that most of the time we trudged through knee-deep snow in open fields. It's amazing, in the pre-dawn darkness and rain, *just how much a haystack piled in a snow field, with a pole sticking up out of it can look like a tank with its gun pointed upward, from a distance. At about seven o'clock in the morning it started to get light, and we found a large cedar grove on the side of a hill that looked as though it would be a good refuge for us while we worked out our plan for the day* [22 December].

'That day was the longest day I have ever spent. At nine o'clock in the morning, we both thought it was about two in the afternoon – that's how long it seemed. We didn't dare sleep, so we just kept patrolling the woods. Looking from the top right hand corner of the woods, we could see German soldiers on the road at an intersection below. They had captured a US light tank, and had one of their own armored cars. Occasionally a German motorcycle rider would go by the road below us...I asked Grant if he would ride with me on the motorcycle if we captured it, he agreed, but we decided that it wouldn't be too smart to travel the roads that way...even if we did get the bike.

'At four o'clock we struck out of the woods and followed the tree line. We had gone about 500 yards over the crest of the hill, when we saw a grouping of three small hamlets in a triangular layout...[Sibret, Villeroux and Chenogne]. *To reach our lines, we would have to pass through at least one of these villages.* [In reality each village was just a grouping of maybe five or six farmhouses.] *We lay by the trees quite a while, and looked the situation over. Remarkably, there seemed to be no movement in the area other than civilian Belgians. We said a prayer and headed down over a long, low, wide-open field, up to the first houses. We walked right up the gravel street, and decided to bluff it out down the main street of Sibret. We must have been a pretty astounding sight. We had our guns slung over our arms like hunters, and all I had on my head was a wool knit cap. (I had lost my helmet when we crossed the river). We met three people in that village, and none of them would tell us anything. "Where Boche?"...but no answers. We didn't ever stop moving, and just kept going right out of the area, with both of us spread apart, trying to cover each other.*

'Finally, I decided that we had had enough luck with the towns and roads, so we took to the open fields again. We went halfway between some very big and dense woods and walked as fast as we could in the snow. We expected any minute to hear a machine gun open up, but by God's grace we were lucky enough

to get by unmolested. Whether the Jerries thought we were some of their own men (Since they were using our uniforms then too), or not, I don't' know.

On the actual approach to our perimeter defence, I knew that we could get shot pretty easily, coming in from the German lines, by our own troops. I remembered that a fellow by the name of Al Putis and his buddy 'Skinny' Combs were the crew on the tank guarding that section of the perimeter. As soon as we got in what I thought was hailing distance, I let out a yell "PUTIS!" There was no answer and I thought maybe the outfit had moved... we kept on going up the road and I yelled again "PUTIS, THIS IS FOSTER WITH GRANT... DON'T YOU GUYS SHOOT US! Sure enough a yell came back...'IS THAT YOU SNAKE?' (My nickname) "YEAH" I shouted. "GET IN HERE, BEFORE YOU GET HURT!" Sweeter words, I've never heard.

'The way we went to get back to our outfit, I figured we travelled about ten kilometers, all in all. After some chow, Grant and I reported our actions and observations to headquarters. We traced our route back on the wall map, and headquarters in turn, pointed out that the dense woods we had so carefully stayed away from was a known concentration of German soldiers and equipment. Later we found out that the German 39th Regiment of the 26th VGD, and supporting armor, had moved into that area just hours before we had decided to break out. So the

A half-track, covered in improvised camouflage, stands guard on one of the approaches to Bastogne

roadblock was well supported.

'*We lost all our vehicles, but Captain McCloskey infiltrated the outer ring of the enemy with most of his troops, and found our trains and Service Battery. He joined Lieutenant-Colonel Creighton W. Abrams (37 Tank Battalion, 4th Armored Division), for the breakthrough to Bastogne a few days later, on 26 December. It was reported that Abrams asked McCloskey what was in the trucks, et al, and Mac answered 'GAS and AMMO'. Abe said, "OK – but stay back – I don't want an explosion in your trucks to harm my column!" The 420th was eventually resupplied and reunited and went on to distinguish itself until war's end in May 1945.*'

Manning a road-block west of Mande St Etienne, Company C from the attached 401st GIR, got completely cut-off from the rest of its unit when elements of Panzer Lehr crossed further down the road and got behind them. With the American infantry, were a small number of tanks. One platoon was detailed off to re-open the road and with the support from a single Sherman, two

Vehicles of the 10th Armored Division camouflaged with white sheets borrowed from citizens of Bastogne.

squads of infantry, one on each side of the road, moved back down the road to where it had been cut. The subsequent fight was brisk and bloody and in a short time German bodies were strewn everywhere. The road was open again with the cost to the Americans of one wounded GI.

During the day of 22 December, the fighting was heaviest on this the southern side of Bastogne, and the town was shelled severely. Because there was no real solid front line the fighting was very confused. Task Force Pyle, now renamed Task Force Watts, the 327th GIR and artillery featured very much in these actions. With mounting casualties and ammunition running low the Germans in their last assault managed to break the American line. Under cover of darkness the GIs fell back to a more defendable line nearer Bastogne.

Manteuffel, Lüttwitz and Kokott were now quite confident that Bastogne would fall. It was obvious to them at that time that the weakest spot was in the west and southwest. Kokott was made responsible for the operation. Without getting the mobile panzer columns from Panzer Lehr involved, he had on hand only his 26th VGD and the attached 901st Panzer Grenadiers, but he had been given extra help in the way of fifteen Panther tanks and more artillery. He had also learned,

through the German Intelligence sources, that there was a considerable amount of US vehicle activity taking place in the Luxembourg area. At last with General Brandenberger's Seventh Army now catching up and giving flank protection from the south, he had no need to worry about any threat from behind in that direction. The 5th Parachute Division from the Seventh Army was now across the Arlon road, north of Martelange, and so could also be counted on to bolster the 26th VGD in their attack on Bastogne, whilst at the same time, watching the south.

It was also on 22 December that Bastogne's greatest moment arrived, one, that would change the town forever.

German Lieutenant General Hasso von Manteuffel was in a confident mood during the fighting around Bastogne.

At about mid-day, under a white flag, a group of four Germans came up the Arlon road from Remoifosse. They came up to the front lines of Company F, 2nd Battalion, 327th GIR. The group was made up of a major, a captain and two enlisted men. The German captain spoke English to a party of GIs, that came out to meet them. He explained that he wished to speak to the commander of Bastogne and had with him an honourable surrender of the town, they were acting as 'parliamentarians'.

The Americans took the four Germans to a house, which was serving as the command post for the weapons platoon of Company F. Here Lieutenant L.E. Smith blindfolded the two German officers, and leaving the two enlisted men there, took the officers over the hill to where Captain J.F McAdams commander of Company F had his command post. He called the 2nd Battalion Headquarters in Marvie, who in turn called Colonel Harper, the Commanding Officer of the 327th Glider Infantry Regiment in Bastogne. The message was then relayed to 101st Headquarters, where word quickly spread that the Germans were going to surrender.

The defenders on hearing this started to relax a little. However, the German note read:

> 'To the USA Commander in the encircled town of Bastogne. The fortune of war is changing. This time, the US forces in and near Bastogne have been encircled by strong German armoured units. More German armoured units have crossed the river Ourthe near Ortheuville, have taken Marche and reached St. Hubert, by passing through Hompre-Sillet-Tillet. Libremont is

The road from Remoifosse. Down this road, towards the American lines, went the German surrender party.

American positions

German Surrender Party under a white flag approached the American defence line

in German hands.

There is only one possibility of saving the encircled USA troops from annihilation. That is the honourable surrender of the encircled town. In order to think it over, a term of two hours shall be granted, beginning with the presentation of this note. If this proposal is rejected, one German artillery corps and six heavy anti-aircraft batteries are ready to annihilate the USA forces in and near Bastogne. The order for firing will be given immediately after the two hours' term.

All serious civilian casualties caused by this artillery fire would not correspond with well-known American humanity.

(signed) The German Commander.'

The ultimatum was handed to McAuliffe by his acting Chief of Staff, Lieutenant-Colonel Ned D Moore. He looked at the paper and said:

'Aw, nuts!'

Civilians being fed by GIs.

McAuliffe tried to give the message serious thought and was trying to write a formal reply when he turned and said:

'What should I say?'

One of his staff, Lieutenant-Colonel H.W.O Kinnard, answered:

'That first remark of yours would be hard to beat.'

'What was that?' McAuliffe asked.

'You said "Nuts"' Laughed Kinnard.

The staff agreed, and had the following reply typed out by a sergeant clerk.

'To the German Commander

NUTS!

The American Commander.'

Colonel J.H Harper, commander of the 327th, was called back and told to deliver the answer to the German party. 'I will deliver it myself, it will be a lot of fun,' said Harper.

He then proceeded back to Company F's command post where the two still blindfolded German officers were waiting. Harper said to them: 'I have the American Commander's reply.' The German captain asked: 'Is it written or verbal?' 'It is written', said Harper. Upon looking at the paper the captain was puzzled, for he had no idea how to translate the one word. He then asked whether the reply was negative or affirmative.

Harper told him:

'The reply is decidedly not affirmative, and if you continue this foolish attack, your losses will be tremendous.'

The two officers were driven back along with Harper, to where the two German enlisted men were waiting. Harper was growing more and more annoyed with the arrogance of the two officers, and just before letting them go through the wire he told them;

'If you don't understand what 'Nuts' means, in plain English it is the same as 'Go to hell.' I will tell you something else – if you continue to attack, we will kill every goddamn German that tries to break into this city.'

They both saluted each other and the German officer gave the parting retort:

'We will kill many Americans, This is war.'

General McAuliffe

97

'On your way, Bud,' said Harper, *'And good luck to you.'*

Something Harper regretted saying for a long time.

This episode boosted the defenders morale no end, and along with it came news that there was to be an airdrop that evening. Also even more heartening news was received. 'Hugh was on his way.' This meant that Patton's 4th Armored Division commanded by Major General Hugh J Gaffey was moving north to help in the relief.

The easy way out for the Germans had gone and Manteuffel was furious

Civilians being treated by American medics.

An American infantry patrol passes a recently hit jeep.

with Lüttwitz for making the surrender terms. He had given no permission for such a demand. To give credence to the threats made by the German surrender party, Manteuffel called on the Luftwaffe to bomb Bastogne that night.

With the Panzer Lehr moving steadily west towards St Hubert the task of reducing Bastogne was left to the 26th VGD. Kokott's attacks from the south-west in the Senonchamps area had not succeeded.

The 26th VGD was positioned around Bastogne as follows: The 78th Grenadier Regiment, front extended from Foy to Marvie; 901 Panzer Grenadier Regiment attached from Panzer Lehr Division, extended from Marvie to the Arlon-Bastogne road; 39th Grenadier Regiment extended from the Arlon-Bastogne road to Senonchamps; 77th Grenadier Regiment extended from Senonchamps to Champs. There were also some reconnaissance units mixed among them. An engineer battalion and a Feld Ersatz (replacement training) battalion were on the northern perimeter.

Manteuffel was now convinced that Bastogne was too strongly defended and decided to contain and invest the town. The combined effects of Bombing and artillery fire coupled with

The water tower on the Route De Marche, then...
...and now.

An American ambulance in the town square awaits casualties being dug out of ruined buildings.

Shell and bomb damage in Bastogne.

A good comparison shot of the edge of the square in Bastogne.

the fact that supplies must be getting short for the beseiged Americans, would soon cause Bastogne to fall into the their hands, or so the Germans reasoned.

The airdrop scheduled for the evening of 22 December did not materialize due to poor visibility. Supplies were now critical within the perimeter. There was a desperate shortage of artillery rounds and medical treatment was rudimentary. The wounded were laid together in whatever shelter could be found. Blankets were scrounged from front line troops to keep them warm. Medics were in very short supply, as was surgical equipment.

But morale remained high. Civilians in the town assisted where they could but were mostly confined to their cellars sheltering from the constant shelling and bombing. It was becoming a puzzle to the men on the receiving end from the

A patrol moves out of Bastogne towards the defence perimeter.

activites of the Luftwaffe just how come they managed to operate in the bad weather when the Allied planes were grounded.

Although in a siege situation, Kokott did mount several more attacks that day. The 39th Volksgrenadier Regiment tried to reduce the little American salient sticking out towards Flamierge in the north-west. Whilst at the same time the 901st Panzer Grenadiers had another go at Team O'Hara at Marvie in the south east. Both attacks failed being repulsed by two regiments of the 327th GIR, who just happened to have been rushed into the two positions a short time earlier.

Captured American equipment was put to good use during the offensive.

The next day 23 December, the weather finally broke, although the ground was covered in snow the day was crisp and clear. It was not long before P47 Thunderbolt's, P38 Lightnings and P51 Mustangs filled the skies. The GIs in foxholes craned their necks in wonderment, as the fighters went to work strafing and bombing German positions. Telltale tracks in the snow led the pilots to their targets.

At about 0900 a pathfinder team dropped into the perimeter between Senonchamps and Bastogne. Their job was to mark the drop zone for the scheduled resupply operation. Men began to search the skies for signs of the C47 transport planes. Sure enough at around 1145 multiple dots in the sky gradually took on the distinctive shapes of the lovable transports. The first drop was made at 1150. In just over four hours 241 planes had parachuted their supplies in. Not all fell within the perimeter, and the miss-aims were greeted eagerly by the Germans who were experiencing their own resupply problems. But, nevertheless, what did get retrieved by the GIs certainly relieved the shortage.

On Christmas Eve things around the Bastogne perimeter

were getting pretty hairy as the defenders, were dangerously over extended. The artillery group in the west was particularly exposed. The attack by the 901st Panzer Grenadiers at Marvie had used up the last counter-attacking force, which consisted of the remnants of Team Cherry. The 327th GIR had been forced back and had to shorten its lines. The tankers were complaining that they had no idea where the airborne troops were positioned and likewise the paratroopers had little idea where the small groups of tanks and tank destroyers were operating.

Colonel Harry W Kinnard, 101st AB G3, decided to regroup his forces into some sort of semblance of order. He re-adjusted the lines so as to give each sector the same amount of defence with troops, tanks and tank destroyers. The line was tightened up to form a circle approximately sixteen miles in circumference.

On the German side, General Lüttwitz had even less to play with. His much depleted 26th VGD and the attached 901st Panzer Grenadiers were struggling to field a force of sufficient effective strength. The 5th Parachute Division to the south was also over extended, and was suffering as a consequence. So much so that Kokott had to send help to seal the line from the threat of American forces coming up from the south. High

C-47s coming in low to drop supplies to the beleagured soldiers and civilians trapped in Bastogne.

Command decided to release their reserve, the 15th Panzer Grenadier Division and the 9th Panzer Grenadier Division. Field Marshal Model, on receiving these fresh divisions, decided that they would be best employed to stiffen the flank between the Fifth and Seventh Armies. As a consequence he could only spare a regiment from the 15th Panzer Grenadier Division to assist Kokott at Bastogne.

Generalmajor Heinz Kokott:

I had my Command Post at Hompre on 23 December 44. Technically speaking, I was in the zone of 5 FS Div [5th

Generalmajor Heinz Kokott

Parachute Division], Seventh Army, which was blocking to the south; however, this was no time to be concerned about boundary lines. The action of 5 FS Div was of vital concern to me. I was facing Bastogne. The American 4th Armored Division drive north threatened my rear. It is an uncomfortable feeling to have someone launching a drive toward your rear; so, boundary or not, 5 FS Div was of constant concern to me. The situation was not aided by my knowledge that 5 FS Div was a very poor division. I feared 4th Armored Division. I knew it was a 'crack' division. Furthermore, Generalmajor Heilmann, Commander of 5 FS Div, was in Lutrebois. He had a very wide front and could not be everywhere. As it happened, I was nearer to this danger point than he; therefore I gave orders to build a resistance line near Chaumont. On 23 December, elements of 14 FS Regiment, 5 FS Division, began to fall back to Hompre. I ordered them to return south and gave them some of my officers. An unknown major in command of four Tiger tanks came into Hompre. I don't know where he came from, or where he was going, but I ordered him south to aid 5 FS Div at Remichampagne and Chaumont.'

The artillery from the German side remained very active, and continued to shell American positions. In reply to this, with beautiful flying weather the P47s went to work once again, strafing the easily identifiable German positions around the entire perimeter.

Late in the day the 115th Kampfgruppe from the 15th Panzer

An Armored infantry division marches up a road. Note height of snow.

Grenadier Division got into its assigned position in the north west sector between Flamierge and Givry. To round the day off, the Luftwaffe made heavy bombing sorties on the town.

Although it was Christmas Eve, there was little seasonal cheer about in the American camp, but at least the airdrops had relieved the stark situation somewhat. The Germans also had far too much to do to concern themselves with thoughts of Christmas cheer and goodwill to all men, for they were planning their major attacks for the 25th.

Generalmajor Heinz Kokott:

'I was to participate in an attack on Bastogne on 25 December, and in preparation, I moved my Command Post to Gives on 24 December. Just before I departed, I left a few guards and directed the placing of some anti-aircraft guns on the heights around Hompre. There was only one good thing about 5 FS Division: it was heavily equipped with weapons. I assisted by giving instructions as to how some of these weapons could be

used to the best advantage. That night I talked to General von Manteuffel on the telephone. I told him that I could not watch two fronts, and that the southern situation was most dangerous. I did not think that 5 FS Division could hold, and I was in no position to prevent a breakthrough. He told me to forget about the American 4th Armored Division, that it was quiet for the moment. The only solution to the problem was to attack Bastogne, he directed that I stop worrying and devote all my efforts to the attack from the northwest. I followed his advice, but the situation was most "disagreeable". It was this situation which precipitated our attack on Bastogne at 0300 on 25 December 1944.'

To the south, Patton's relieving forces were well on the way in their northwards drive. With the 26th and 80th Infantry Divisions to the right and the 4th Armored Division on the left, the plan was for these divisions to clear a corridor almost twenty-four miles wide, the distance between the Luxembourg border and the Neufchateau-Bastogne highway.

The infantry had it tough, trying to protect the right flank of the 4th Armored Division. The countryside consisted of heavily wooded steep ravines, with very few roads. The only good thing was that the Germans in this area were unprepared for any attacks from a southerly direction. It was different at the head of the 4th Armored Division, for the German 5th Parachute Division had arrived in force and was now deploying.

At around mid-afternoon on 22 December, CCA of the 4th Armored Division, was just outside the town of Martelange. There to meet them was a company from the German 5th Parachute Division, which for the rest of the day stopped the Americans from securing the two already demolished bridges across the River Sure. It would take the Armored Infantry until well after midnight to finally reach the far bank and secure the area. Engineers arrived and claimed that the banks were too steep for them to erect a pontoon or treadway bridge, and that it would require a Bailey bridge, but this would not be completed until the following afternoon.

CCB to the left of CCA was progressing north on minor roads, it had encountered some small-arms fire as it drew level with Martelange, but it managed to sweep this aside and carry on. When it reached the village of Burnon it too had to stop to allow engineers to re-build a demolished bridge.

In the early hours of 23 December, CCB resumed its attack, but only got as far as the village of Chaumont. There, waiting for them was another company from the German 5th Parachute Division. The American attack went in – infantry supported by tanks. However, the armored infantry ended up having to go it alone as the tanks were unable to get a grip on the muddy slopes. After heavy fighting in Chaumont, much of it house to house, the American infantrymen finally evicted the German paratroopers from the village. With the Germans were a group of Tiger tanks, sent south by Kokott to protect his southern flank. These tanks created havoc amongst the bogged down Shermans and destroyed many.

By 24 December, CCA had got beyond the River Sure, but was only as far as the next village, which was Warnach. Still over nine miles from Bastogne, and CCB was still fighting around Chaumont, as it desperately tried to rid the place of the German assault guns and tank destroyers, which were taking

Soldiers of the 9th Armored Division help local children celebrate Christmas.

their toll. There was to be no Christmas present relief for the beleaguered troops at Bastogne as all had hoped.

During the evening of Christmas Eve, all in the town of Bastogne detected the sound of aeroplane engines, the beat was totally different from the American noise. Within minutes flares illuminated the town and bombs rained down from low flying Junkers 88s. The planes made two runs and heavily damaged the town, especially the area around the square which took the full force. It was left looking like a wasteland. The aid station of the 10th Armored Division CCB was also hit. Wounded were pulled from the burning building, but many perished when it totally collapsed. It was not a pleasant task digging out the debris to get to the bodies.

Christmas day found the 'Battling Bastards of Bastogne', as they now called themselves, still smarting from the overnight bombing. For many it had been the first time they had been on the receiving end of the Luftwaffe.

Generalmajor Kokott had been promised the entire 15th Panzer Grenadier Division to aid his all-out assault on the town that day. In fact, he only got one regiment, but with attached assault guns, Mark IVs and Panther tanks, it was a force to be reckoned with. Along with one of Kokott's *Volksgrenadier* Regiments taken from the 26th VGD the force took its place ready for the coming attack. They were hoping to break through the American lines west of Bastogne in two places simultaneously. One at the village of Champs, the other in the area of the 327th GIR between Champs and the main Marche road.

Ludwig Lindemann

'One of the last big offensives in the direction of Bastogne in which we were involved, along with other units, occurred at a place called Flamierge, north-west of Bastogne. At the briefing for the offensive, officers and ncos of our three Kompanies (9th, 10th and 11th) were addressed by the Battalion Kommander, Hauptmann Raab. During the briefing Raab turned to me and said, "My dear Lindemann, we have known each other from Russia, from the Raab combat team at the Vistula, and also here in the Ardennes, and it is my decision that you will be Kompany Führer for these offensives. So, good luck then!" Today I still have those words in my ears.

The next morning we assembled ready to move off. I gave the

German troops moving forward during an assault. Note the soldier with the recently introduced assault rifle – the M44 *Sturmgewehr*.

command and the 10th Kompany took the lead and set off marching to the start line. Because of the losses we had suffered we were severely understrength. We reached the advance positions of the battalion, at the place called Flamierge, without incurring casualties. At the entrance to the village we came across an American jeep in full working order and put it to good use. We took up our assigned positions in readiness for the coming assault on Bastogne and awaited the order to advance. In the very early hours of Christmas morning the white clad Germans moved out. The *Volksgrenadiers* were quickly inside Champs, but the surprised 502nd PIR fought back, the fighting was intense, much of it hand to hand. Two battalions of *Panzergrenadiers*, one on foot and the other riding tanks crashed into the 327th GIR positions.

The tanks got through the American lines and were on their

A Pz MkIV wrecked by concentrated American fire-power during the Christmas day attack.

way to the village of Hemroulle, almost on the outskirts of Bastogne itself. One of the advancing panzers radioed Kokott's headquarters to say they had made it to Bastogne, but in fact it had not, as the crew had got confused and mistook Hemroulle for Bastogne. The tanks ranged behind the American lines inside the perimeter, threatening the 502nd and 327th command posts. After heavy fighting and superb shooting from units of the 705th Tank Destroyer Battalion the German tanks were eventually destroyed. The eleven tanks that actually got into Hemroulle were hit from all sides as a rain of red-hot steel met them. The tanks were so badly hit by such a variety of weaponry, that it was difficult to spot who did what.

Robert M.Bowen, Company C, 401st Glider Infantry, 101st Airborne Division;

'December 24 and 25, 1944 were for me two of the worst days of my life. The 101st Airborne Division had been surrounded at Bastogne since the night of the 20th, was short of ammunition and supplies, had its hospital captured, and was in danger of being overrun. I was an NCO rifle platoon leader in Company

C, 401 GIR and my company was manning roadblocks on the western perimeter of the encircled city near Flamierge.

We had repulsed attacks in our sector on the 19th, 20th and 22nd. On the 23rd the Germans came again early in the morning out of a heavy fog which hung over the bitter cold, snow covered hills, wearing snowsuits and with tanks painted white. They were from the 77th Regiment of the 26th Volksgrenadier Division, fourteen tanks with infantry. Although the roadblock had a Sherman, a Tank Destroyer, a half-track and a 37mm anti-tank gun, a combination of misfortunes prevented their being much use. The Sherman was knocked out in the first burst of shelling, the anti-tank gun was frozen in the ground and couldn't be traversed to fire on the enemy armor and the crew of the half-track vanished. There was little support from division artillery because of an ammunition shortage, but our 81mm mortars were a big help. The division history devoted two short paragraphs to the action, making it sound no more than a patrol incident: nothing about the desperation, hopelessness and drama of the men who fought and died there that day. I was wounded about 1600 and put in a basement of a house just behind the main line of resistance where the medics had set up an aid station. The roadblock fell just after dark. All the wounded and medics, the crews of the armor and a few men from Company C were captured, all that remained of the reinforced platoon that held the position. The prisoners were thoroughly searched, threatened with death, and finally marched to trucks which took them into St.Hubert for interrogation. When that was over they were put in the attic of a nearby house under the guard of young Gefreiters with itchy trigger fingers. We were hustled out of the house early the next morning to a captured American weapons carrier with an attached trailer. A biting wind blew over the chilling snow, piercing our inadequate clothing like a knife. We were hungry, cold, and depressed: hungry because we had been living off one or two K rations a day for nearly a week: cold because many of us did not have overcoats, overshoes, gloves or mufflers: and depressed because after fighting debilitating campaigns in Normandy and Holland with their high casualty rates, this one in Belgium threatened to be the last straw to push us over the edge. The medics and wounded were put in the weapons carrier with a guard and driver, the rest somehow jammed in the trailer and we started down the main street in a north-easterly direction. The town was flooded with German troops and tanks, all going in the direction of Bastogne. Perhaps they were the same ones which would overrun Company C on that very night, losing all eighteen tanks and hundreds of panzer and Volksgrenadiers in a futile attempt to take the city. Once we left the city we could see the carnage left by the German offensive. Burning villages, wrecked and burning tanks, trucks and smaller vehicles. Corpses, American and German, bloody, sprawled grotesquely in many instances on the whipped snow, ignored by small bands of refugees which wandered about like lost children. In the distance toward Bastogne could be heard the dull explosion of crashing shellfire and the rumble of German artillery. As it was still overcast and foggy, and had been ever since we got to Belgium, there were no planes in this sector. The wretched ride took hours with the driver nearly becoming lost despite having a map. The sky began to clear and in the distance could be heard the dull murmur of plane engines. We came to a small village finally, one that had been recently bombed and strafed by our fighter planes. Houses were ablaze, walls knocked in by bombs, German soldiers with terror-stricken faces still lay in roadside ditches. Rescuers were going through the houses searching for victims. The wounded were taken from the weapons carrier and into a field hospital just about the time our planes came back. The Germans shouted 'Ya-boes! Der Teufel! Der Teufel! Every able man rushed outside, firing every weapon available at the screaming, diving, bullet spitting planes. We in the operating room huddled on the floor as bullets splintered the walls. Happy in one way that the weather had cleared but sad in another that one of those.50 caliber bullets could kill us. After being treated, the wounded were taken to a nearby barn which held the rest of the POWs plus some other Americans who had been picked up along the way. The floor was ankle deep in wet, urine soaked straw and cow manure. Soon more POWs were brought in, air corps men who had just been shot down in supply runs over Bastogne. Once more everyone was interrogated and returned to the barn which by now was so crowded that it looked like a Tokyo subway train. The guards took several men to a nearby kitchen and they returned with two kettles of steaming noodle soup. As only the airborne guys had any eating utensils, the ever present spoon, these were passed around and everyone got something to eat. Then the guards told us through one of the

GI prisoners being marched to the rear during the German advance in the Ardenne.

POWs who spoke a little German that straw was available to put on the floor for sleeping. That was impossible. There was hardly room to stand without bumping into someone. Most of us sat or stood all night. Christmas Day was dismal for all of us. Cold, tired and hungry we were led from the barn and lined up in a column on the road with five German guards toting machine pistols. We walked all morning on the icy road, frosty breath preceding us. We passed more wrecked vehicles, one an ambulance full of corpses and still on fire. Cars sometimes littered the road and the POWs were made to drag them to the ditches. Feeling quite superior, some of the guards made the prisoners carry their bulky rucksacks. A stocky, middle aged guard with a broad face walked just by my side. He had gotten a ration of fried chicken and as he walked along he waved pieces under my nose saying: 'Das is gut, Ja?' Then he would take a bite. His contemptible conduct didn't last long. Suddenly the sound of plane motors came over nearby trees. 'Yarboes,' the guards screamed. We dove for the ditches, all but my taunting guard, as the P-47s skimmed the tree tops on the right and came barrelling towards us with guns blazing. The ditches were shallow, not deep enough to hide our bodies. Even though I buried myself in the snow, I could follow the paths of the .50 caliber shells as they raced across the field and hit the road, showering us with debris and sparks. The planes were past in an instant, made a wide arc and were back again. A brave medic got to his knees and waved his arms as more bullets tore up the road. It worked. The planes levelled off and left. I was shaking all over. The bullets had barely missed my head as they tracked across the road. The taunting guard lay in a widening pool of blood, the chicken leg still grasped in his hand.

Technical Sergeant Bonner, one of the medics who came up to help the wounded at our road block was down, a bullet through his hip. It was serious. The guards reorganized us, threatening us with their machine pistols. Bringing the dead and wounded along, we started off once again, but didn't get far. Another flight of P-47s spotted us and came barrelling for the road. We scattered like pins in a bowling alley. The planes made two passes and left. Perhaps they recognized our uniforms or were after better targets. We started off again more wary than ever. Soon a small village came into sight. The POWs were taken to a building which must have been the headquarters for a Nazi party unit, it was so filled with photos, flags and other propaganda material. Our medics immediately tended the wounded, but Tech/Sgt Bonner was beyond their limited facilities. They begged the guards to have him removed to a local hospital. The guards refused at first, but later recanted. We were served a meal, a box of dried up apples, two per man. We sat quietly on the hardwood flooring, nibbling at the apples and watching Bonner in his agony.

It was close to dark when the guards came and took away all the wounded. The hospital was a makeshift affair, a convent which had been converted to handle wounded until they could be moved to the rear. Straw pallets on the floor served as beds and there were gray woollen blankets for covers. I was put in a room with a dozen or so Germans, all of whom had been operated on for frostbite and frozen limbs. Most were in great pain. I was put between two Waffen SS troopers who, at first, eyed me with hatred in their eyes. However, after a while one became friendly and even offered me a stub of a cigarette from a small metal box he carried in a shirt pocket. He spoke no English and I no German so communication was rough. I did learn that he was an anti-tank gunner and destroyed several Ami tanks before a shell hit his gun and killed everyone but him. Catholic sisters acted as nurses, helping the doctors and serving meals. On Christmas evening everyone got a bowl of steaming stew and later the sister gave everyone a piece of chocolate. Somewhere down the hall, I could hear feminine voices singing Christmas carols. Even though they were in German, the music was familiar. While they sang the beautiful songs, Tech/Sgt Bonner died. He came to save us at the road block. He died in the effort. Perhaps there was some correlation between his death and the Christmas story.'

An action in the above area as described by a platoon sergeant. The platoon had fled from the courtyard of the 401st Bn. HQ when word had been received of enemy tanks approaching. Now they were on their way back, determined to take on the enemy tanks and troops. The sergeant wrote:

'We were half way back to the farmhouse (CP) and I might add we were downright cocky about our chances of taking on all those German tanks, then, out of nowhere two 705 TD's showed up in the woods with us. Soon after that we went all the way back to within 200 yards and there sat four of the Jerry's tanks with their infantry milling around the farm house. This had all happened within thirty minues at the most. The time could have been 0800. We were all engaged in a dead serious act now. Some

German dead after their Christmas day attack.

of the Jerries were cooking their breakfast and we caught them by surprise. They had made the mistake of not coming after us, and, at least they should have been ready for a counter-attack. We all opened up at once. We poured all the rifle fire into that old farmhouse. Suddenly, all four tanks took off going straight north, down the road toward Champs, one right behind the other. Now they were on the run, as if they were only saving the tanks. The German infantrymen ran out from the farmhouse in a rush to catch a ride on the tanks. Many of them were cut down by our rifle fire, which now had become a cross-fire of 2nd, 1st and 3rd Platoons of Company C.

'I was walking along near the edge of the clearing in line with the potato pile. Walking next to me among the large hardwood trees was Staff Sergeant Don Williams. He was a platoon Sergeant in Company C of the 705 TD Battalion. Two of his TDs were following along behind us at a slow pace. The Connecticut platoon Sergeant asked me to hold up my men while he taught the Germans a small lesson in tank warfare. Sergeant Tony D'Angelo from Wellsville, Ohio, was the tank commander of the TD nearest me. He was out of his TD walking in front leading his tank around the big trees. Tony stopped his driver right beside me. I heard him say to his gunner inside, "Take the last tank first and then one at a time right up the line. Fire when ready." He fired point blank into the side of each MK IV enemy tank. The last tank first, and so on down the line, was hit and caught fire. The TD next to me (D'Angelo) fired six shots. Two shots hit the big trees, four shots hit tanks and four were knocked out. It was absolutely the best that I ever saw.'

Yet once again, as with Neffe, the Germans had nearly succeeded. So near, yet so far.

Kokott's units were becoming a spent force and, as a result, he would be unable to make any more concerted attacks. He now faced south knowing that a large American armored force was barrelling down on him from that direction. He had also got word that the American tanks were almost in the village of Hompre, not four miles away. Kokott decided to send a now much depleted battalion of the 39th Regiment to the village of Assenois to block the advance of the American relief force.

CHAPTER FIVE

RELIEF OF BASTOGNE

Kokott tried one more attack on the morning of 26 December. His troops to the west of Bastogne were holding a small salient along the main road from Mande St Etienne. He got together a small assault group from his 26th VGD, with an attachment of ten tank destroyers and sent them in a north-easterly direction towards Hemroulle. This, he hoped, would bring the assault group round for an attack on the town from the north. It was not to be. It did manage to form a wedge through the lines of the 327th GIR, but was then caught in the open by the massed American artillery situated west of Bastogne and was literally blown to pieces.

Four tank destroyers managed to evade the deluge of fire but were caught out by a large ditch on the outskirts of Hemroulle, where they too were destroyed. This was to be the final German assault on the town of Bastogne. By that afternoon, at Kokott's command post, more bad news arrived. The 5th Parachute Division had crumbled and his 39th Regiment was under heavy

A knocked out *Sturmgeschütz* tank destroyer.

Street scene in Bastogne.

attack from the south. Kokott had no reserves left to send to their assistance. In the late afternoon he got a report from his 39th Regiment saying that American tanks had broken through the German positions at Assenois.

With pleas of help bombarding him, Field Marshall Model told the dwindling German forces to hold the Americans inside the perimeter until aid could be sent.

The force that broke through Assenois was in fact Combat Command Reserve of the 4th Armored Division. With CCA and CCB of that division being held up, CCR had been committed. It had been ordered up to Neufchateau on Christmas Eve. From there it had started its attack up the main road. It was not long before units of CCR encountered stiff resistance while

approaching Sibret. Its commander Colonel Wendell Blanchard decided to swing CCR off the main road and onto a secondary road where the resistance might be lighter.

The little village of Remichampagne was cleared, and by about mid-afternoon Lieutenant-Colonel Creighton W. Abrams commander of the 37th Tank Battalion, and the 53rd Armored Infantry Battalion under Lieutenant-Colonel George L Jaques was on the outskirts of the next village, Clochimont.

The two commanders stood at a junction discussing the plan for the attack on Sibret from that direction, when to the north they spotted C47 aircraft dropping supplies to the besieged troops. Without telling their commander they decided to plunge through Assenois and open a corridor through to Bastogne. Abrams called up Captain William A Dwight with Company C, 37th Tank Battalion and Company C, 53rd AIB. Abrams briefed Dwight on his plan and sent him on his way. At 1620, 26 December, 1st Lieutenant Charles P Boggess, leading the point, with eight Shermans set off. Artillery saturated Assenois in a pre-arranged bombardment. On reaching the village, Boggess called for the shelling to lift. Without waiting for a reply he tore through the village as Germans began to emerge from their cellars. The armored infantry behind became engaged in hand-to-hand fighting, whilst Boggess careered out the other side of Assenois, but with only five tanks, as three had become lost in the streets. Somehow or other an infantry half-track had attached itself to Boggess's column and had slotted itself in between tanks number 3 and 4.

It did not take Boggess long to reach the top of the hill leading to Bastogne, but the half-track had developed engine trouble and was struggling to keep up. It gradually fell behind

121

Looking out for snipers in a Belgian village.

Tanks of the 4th Armored Division ready for action south of Bastogne.

Sherman and Stuart tanks on the move.

holding up the tanks in its wake. A gap had formed in the column, which gave the Germans at the side of the road time enough to lay some anti-tank mines. The half-track reached this spot and hit one. Captain Dwight was in the tank immediately behind the disabled half-track and ordered it moved. Once the road was cleared Dwight led his column at full speed up the hill to catch up. Meanwhile Boggess had reached the plateau and spotted in the snow covered fields camouflaged parachutes. He also spotted a bunker amidst some pine trees. His tank immediately fired three shells at it, while his machine-gunner mowed down a group of Germans in the trees.

General McAuliffe had been informed about the relief, and in turn had told the 326th Airborne Engineers, who were holding that particular part of the perimeter, to be on the lookout. They spotted the tanks but were not sure of the identity of them through all the murk.

Boggess saw a little further on from the bunker, a line of manned foxholes either side of the road and was convinced this was the 101st Airborne's position. He stopped his tank and shouted:

'Come out here, this is the 4th Armored Division.'

After a minute or two a GI got out of his hole and introduced himself.

'2nd Lieutenant Webster – 326th Engineer Battalion – 101st Airborne.'

The time was 16.45. More GIs greeted Boggess and asked for water and three jerrycans were found for them. To the GIs it was delicious when compared to melted snow they'd been forced to drink.

Captain Dwight moved on to the southern outskirts of Bastogne and met McAuliffe. Dwight introduced himself as the advanced guard, 4th Armored Division. McAuliffe replied, 'I am really glad to see you.' Twenty minutes later Abrams arrived in Bastogne.

At 1830, while the fighting was still going on in Assenois, an infantry unit using half-tracks headed for Bastogne. But the Germans had regained control of the area around the bunker and ambushed the column. Three half-tracks were destroyed by panzerfausts. In the darkness the Americans cleared up the place and by midnight all was quiet again.

German prisoners from the 26th Volksgrenadier Division being brought in to Bastogne.

Airborne troops moving up a fire break.

Generalmajor **Heinz Kokott:**
'The 39th Grenadier Regiment had its principle strength in Assenois, Salvacourt, and Sibret. I told Kaufmann to continue facing towards Bastogne, and not to form a front to the south. I warned him, of course, to watch his rear and, when it became worse, to prepare an all-around defence, using all his anti-tank guns.

When the US 4th Armored Division broke into Assenois in the afternoon, Kaufmann called me. He said there were twelve enemy tanks in the village. The tanks were through Assenois and going to Bastogne. I knew it was all over. I told Kaufmann just to block the road. The corridor was still very small, the width of the road itself, and I hoped that with road-blocks and barriers, we could close the ring around Bastogne. It was a difficult task, however, because 39th Grenadier Regiment had been scattered on both sides of the road by 4th Armored Division tanks, which

German dead around Bastogne.

were firing in all directions. Now it was difficult for 39th Grenadier Regiment to fight back without firing at each other. We tried to get reinforcements there, but the troops of the 26th VGD were so tired from their fighting that they couldn't make the effort. The Führer Begleit Brigade was ordered by Corps to move to Sibret to close the circle, but it didn't get there in time. When it arrived, the US 4th Armored Division had already taken Sibret.'

A lifeline now existed to the outside world for the 'Battling Bastards of Bastogne,' It was only a narrow corridor through the German lines but it was enough to get the much needed supplies and men through to the besieged town.

Under the immortal sign, General Taylor Commander of the 101st Airborne Division shakes the hand of the top brass.

CHAPTER SIX

END OF THE BULGE

By 22 December, the 2nd Panzer Division was well on its way to the Meuse. It had avoided any American strong-points on its high speed dash to its assigned objective. It was however, caught a few times by Allied air strikes, which were beginning to take their toll. The division was now just like a finger protruding in a northwestward direction. Its column stretching back just over seven miles and with its lead units being probed all the time by Allied patrols. There were no units to guard its flanks: Panzer Lehr to its south had just secured the town of Rochefort, and General Bayerlein had decided to rest his exhausted troops for a time before pressing on. To the north, the 116th Panzer Division was finding the going tough trying to cut the main Marche-Hotton highway. They had come up against defences of the newly arrived American 84th Infantry Division

Infantry from the US 84th Infantry Division move out to attack the 116th Panzer Division which had slowed down in its drive westward.

and had stalled. So much so that von Manteuffel decided to go personally and see its commander, General von Waldenburg, to roust him into renewed efforts to get the job done.

German reinforcements, by way of 9th Panzer and the rest of the 15th Panzer Grenadiers were held at bay by the ever-increasing sorties of the Allied airforce.

General Heinrich von Lüttwitz:

'On 21 December 44, the reconnaissance group of 2nd Panzer Division was located in Tenneville. Although I wanted the reconnaissance group to move fast through the Bois de Bande and reach Bande on that day, I could not order the movement because the weight of the Division was too strung out to follow. It extended all the way back from Tenneville to Bourcy. The 2nd Panzer Division later reported to me that there was a road block held by strong enemy forces in front of Tenneville. On the 23-24 December 44, I personally drove up to the point of the Division and discovered that the road block consisted only of thin barricades. I saw that there were no enemy forces and later had to clear the matter by a court-martial. I then got the Division moving, but we had proceeded northwest only a short distance when we came to a small river crossing. At that place, the whole road was blown up. It was an exceptionally good piece of work by the American engineers. We reconnoitred a bypass and the Division then moved rapidly on to Marche.'

By 24 December, the 2nd Panzer Division was getting very low on fuel and requested permission to withdraw from its hazardous surroundings to a better defensive line. Lüttwitz agreed as he could see clearly the predicament his armoured forces were in. Hitler refused the request. The Division's forward unit was now only four miles from its objective, the River Meuse, it occupied two areas, one around Foy-Notre-Dam and the other around Celles and Conjoux. Virtually out of fuel, they dug in and waited for the inevitable American attack. A message arrived from Field Marshal Model telling the division, if it had no more fuel then it was to proceed to the Meuse on foot. Nobody paid any attention. The men had had enough, besides it was Christmas Day.

At first no attacks materialized and Major General Ernest N Harmon's 2nd Armored Division was sent to cover the area in front of the 2nd Panzer Division's line of advance; there he was ordered to take up defensive positions. The whole of the American VII Corps, to which the 2nd Armored belonged, had been ordered south from the Aachen area to counter-attack the Germans.

Harmon was at dinner on 23 December, when he was interrupted by an officer from his division bearing news that one of his reconnaissance patrols had been fired on by German tanks less than ten miles to the south. Harman was galvanized into action, he sent a force of tanks south-eastward to meet the oncoming threat.

Leading the American column was a task force under the command of Lieutenant-Colonel Hugh R O'Farrell. It had a jeep out front the crew of which heard the clanking of tank tracks and the sound of voices. The jeep was immediately turned around and proceeded up the column telling the drivers of the vehicles and troops to quietly take cover in the trees lining the road. The night was illuminated by a full moon and, with snow on the ground, visibility was very good. The German vehicles rumbled on totally unaware of the presence of American troops and ran into the ambush. American tankers opened up with everything they had and within minutes of opening fire had reduced the German vehicles to burning hulks. It had been a roving patrol on the northern flank of the main panzer column, which was advancing on Celles.

Harman called VII Corps headquarters with news he had got from some local Belgians. 'They say the Krauts are out of gas. They're sitting ducks.' After much haggling he was finally given

Panzer MkVs, Panthers, halted in the Bulge through lack of fuel.

permission to attack. It was Christmas morning, and he sent his CCB southwest towards Celles and his CCA southeast to Rochefort to cut the bottom of the German finger. The two forces, without too much trouble, finally linked on 26 December cutting off 2nd Panzer Division from the rest of the German forces. With the aid of RAF rocket firing Typhoon aircraft the pocket was cleared. It seemed to the men of 2nd Panzer that the whole area was crawling with tanks.

Panzer Lehr tried to break through but got the same reception. Counter-attack after counter-attack by the Germans to try and reopen the route to Celles failed. The 116th Panzer Division also tried to fight through but was stopped dead by the 84th Infantry Division at Verdenne. It dug in, but was finished as an assault division. The other German division sent there, 9th Panzer, managed to seize and control the road junction at Humain, just northeast of Rochefort. But it too was pounded by artillery and tanks of the surrounding 2nd Armored Division and was forced into submission. Lüttwitz, hearing of the disaster, ordered his columns to fall back on Rochefort leaving the men trapped in the pocket to their own devices. That night Manteuffel gave the order for the men to try and break out on foot. Not many made it. The German high water mark had been reached and the westward drive had been finally stopped.

Hitler, upon learning of the destruction of his units, reluctantly consented to a withdrawal of German forces to more defensible positions. But he had by no means given up on his original plan. He insisted to Manteuffel that he should clear up the Bastogne salient, before renewing the drive for the Meuse and finally on to Antwerp.

The Bastogne area would see many more days of heavy fighting. The place seemed to suck both German and American units into it like a magnet. The American plan was for the U.S 3rd Army to attack towards Bastogne. To the west of the narrow corridor two divisions the 11th Armored Division and the 87th Infantry Division were to head north and come up alongside the defenders in the Champs area. At the same time the 35th Infantry Division was to drive up towards Longvilly. This would widen the relief corridor and drive a wedge into the German positions. Attack date was 30 December.

The attack started and met head on with the German forces hell bent on cutting the corridor from east to west. The 11th

This German half-track has caught a direct hit.

Armored Division and 87th Infantry Division were hit by elements of Panzer Lehr and 26th VGD, which had been regrouping around the Bastogne area. The US 35th Infantry Division in the east hit the 1st SS Panzer Division full on. The attacks bogged down with no one going anywhere. The Americans had not succeeded in widening the corridor and the Germans had not cut it.

The battle fell into a slogging match with ever increasing casualties on both sides. To top it all the weather was deteriorating rapidly. This trend would continue well into the New Year, with major German attacks still hitting the exhausted defenders of Bastogne.

Things finally started to change when, on 31 December, Hitler threw in a quickly conceived attack way down south in the Vosges Mountain region. In theory a mini Ardennes attack, with a view of nipping off the thin American salient there and surrounding Strasbourg. In his mind Hitler knew the Americans would have to send reinforcements to that area so reducing the numbers around Bastogne. It was not a success, the German units were below strength and ill equipped, and the American determination was such that it thwarted all attempts to break through. The Germans were now a spent force, and with a seeming never ending supply of fresh US divisions arriving daily there seemed little hope of any success.

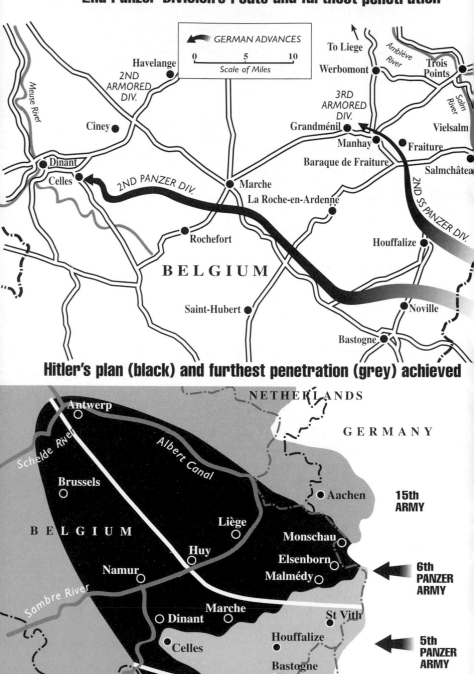

2nd Panzer Division's route and furthest penetration

GERMAN ADVANCES

Scale of Miles
0   5   10

Meuse River

Havelange
2ND ARMORED DIV.

To Liege

Werbomont

Amblève River

Trois Points

Salm River

Ciney

3RD ARMORED DIV.

Grandménil

Vielsalm

Dinant

Manhay

Fraiture

Celles

Baraque de Fraiture

Salmchâtea

2ND PANZER DIV.

Marche

La Roche-en-Ardenne

2ND SS PANZER DIV.

Rochefort

Houffalize

BELGIUM

Saint-Hubert

Noville

Bastogne

Hitler's plan (black) and furthest penetration (grey) achieved

NETHERLANDS

GERMANY

Antwerp

Schelde River

Albert Canal

Brussels

Aachen

15th ARMY

BELGIUM

Liège

Monschau

Huy

Elsenborn

Namur

Malmédy

6th PANZER ARMY

Sambre River

Marche

St Vith

Dinant

Celles

Houffalize

5th PANZER ARMY

Bastogne

7th ARMY

FRANCE

Meuse River

Echternach

LUXEMBOURG

The Luftwaffe's last offensive, Operation BODENPLATTE, took place 1 January 1945. Allied airfields in Holland Belgium and Luxembourg were attacked. Although some 800 Allied aircraft were damaged or destroyed German losses were also heavy and the Luftwaffe never recovered. Here Hitler and Göring listen to General Heinz Guderian as he indicates some aspect of the planned air assault. *Top:* A Focke Wolfe 190 is prepared for take-off in the winter of 1945.

An American jeep enters Houffalize.

War torn Houffalize after the battle.

The Luftwaffe on 1 January made its final attempt of the war to swing the balance. Over 1,000 fighters and fighter bombers took off to destroy Allied forward fighter bases in the hope of ruling the skies again. Although it did inflict much damage to Allied aircraft caught on the ground, the cost to itself was also high. Many German planes were shot down and precious, experienced pilots lost. So much so, it too became a spent force and never really showed itself in any real strength for the remaining months of the war.

On 3 January 1945, the British commander, Field Marshall Montgomery, was put in charge of the northern sector of the Ardennes. He commenced his drive south with the American 1st Army and British XXX Corps. On 9 January the 4th Armored Division and the 101st Airborne Division struck out of the Bastogne perimeter towards Houffalize. By 15 January the northern and southern Allied forces were within sight of each other and on 16 January, one month after the initial German assault, the two forces linked up at Houffalize, effectively trapping the exhausted, disease ridden German forces within the Allied pincers.

The Germans that could make it, retreated eastwards, back to their homeland, harassed all the while by pursuing tanks and fighter aircraft.

The German forces were in retreat.

Ludwig Lindemann

For most of the time during the fighting-withdrawal I was leading the 10th Kompanie, during which time we were almost completely wiped out. In the village of Bertogne I came face to face with a Sherman tank and managed to put it out of action when I fired at it from a stable window. There were other German troops in the village retreating to the German border and I recall meeting up with an Oberleutnant Sural and immediately struck up a brief friendship. We each led our units off eastward, became separated, and never saw each other again. Did he ever make it to safety and survive the war? We passed through Bertogne, Longchamps, Recogne, Longville, Oberwampach and headed north from Hosingen to a village over the German border. Next we went to Karlshausen back to where we had started. It was here that my runner and I ate a proper meal for the first time in weeks. During the periods of heavy fighting we had rarely seen food rations. We often ate snow and, due to this, had violent diarrhoea.'

Hitler's dream of re-capturing the port of Antwerp and thus driving a wedge between the mainly British and American forces had experienced some limited success. Without him realizing it his WACHT AM RHEIM offensive had created a rift among the leaders within the Allied camp, one that would never really be healed for the remainder of the war.

Bernard Law Montgomery

Montgomery had sent a letter to Eisenhower on the 29 December asking that he be put in charge of all Allied troops in the west. To Eisenhower, Montgomery's letter seemed to read that his judgement in making General Bradley overall commander was a bad one, and that he, Eisenhower, was not up to the job.

Eisenhower was furious and was in the process of drafting a letter to the US Army Chief of Staff, General Marshall, in the United States, saying they would have to choose between him and Montgomery. Before it was sent Montgomery's Chief of Staff, Major General Sir Frances de Guingand, got wind of the rift and stalled Eisenhower's headquarters saying that he would talk to the unsuspecting Montgomery about the implications of his letter. Montgomery, when he realized what he had unintentionally implied, wrote back to Eisenhower apologizing and ending the note with, 'Very distressed that my letter may have upset you and I would ask you to tear it up'. (He subsequently sought to reassure Eisenhower of his total support whatever his plans.) Eisenhower was reasonably happy with this and decided not to carry the matter further.

However, it was not quite the end of the matter, on 7 January Montgomery decided to hold a press conference, ironically as a gesture of goodwill between American and British forces. Unfortunately, it all came out wrong, and the way Montgomery put it over sounded as if he had saved the day and masterminded all the defensive and offensive moves. Of course the British press played on this misinterpretation and blew it all out of proportion saying things like 'Montgomery had foreseen the attack and had saved the Americans'. Once again the two factions were at each other's throats and, once again, Montgomery had to write a pacifying letter, this time to General Bradley, saying that it had been a great honour for him to have served with such fine American troops and commanders.

It took Sir Winston Churchill, two weeks later in the House of Commons, to put things right. He stated that the battle in the Ardennes was primarily an American battle:

'The Americans have engaged thirty or forty men for every one we have engaged and they have lost sixty to eighty men for every one of us. It was the greatest American battle of the war and will, I believe, be regarded as an ever famous American victory.'

Although the Battle was an Anglo-American affair it will invariably be viewed as strictly American. When it boils down to it the men from all sides at the 'sharp end' would not care what was happening above them. All that mattered to the German Grenadier, American GI or British Tommy was that they survive the

Churchill put the record straight regarding involvement of British and American troops during what was coming to be known as the Battle of the Bulge.

137

The fighting is all over and this German soldier, his leg almost blown off, receives aid from a medic of the 10th Armored Division.

living hell of battle and the atrocious weather conditions that they had to endure.

As you can imagine, this was not an easy battle to condense, and keep simple. The lines were very fluid, and covered a vast sector, with much of the fighting going on simultaneously. However, I hope that, with the aid of this guide, you will be able to tour round and see the main areas of interest. Above all, spare some thoughts for the men who were there in that freezing winter of 1944/45.

A memorial ceremony for the men of Company C 9th Armored Engineer Battalion 9th Armored Division, who were killed during the seige of Bastogne – held 22 January 1945.

Major Charles L. Hustead delivers his address to the people of Bastogne

Major Charles Hustead and his wife presenting packages of nuts to the children of Bastogne. (1948)

At a review, Major General William H. Morris Commander of the 10th Armored Division and Major General Anthony C. McAuliffe (front row) prepare to take the salute.

CCB 10th Armored Division being presented with the Presidential Unit Citation for their part in the defense of Bastogne.

CHAPTER SEVEN

THE GUIDE

Because of the nature of the battle the actual battlefield tour covers some considerable distance. Your own transport is a must.

There is public transport in the area, in the way of buses, but these will not take you to the actual spots. Also the tourer would have to catch several buses just to get to one particular village. Bastogne railway station has been closed for some time and consequently travel by rail is out of the question. To get to this part of Europe it is best to use your car. There are airports in Brussels, Luxembourg and Cologne and then you will have to hire a vehicle on arrival. Obviously Brussels and Luxembourg are the nearest cities to the area covered in this guide.

From the ferry port of **Ostende**, take the main highway, number **E40**, and head for **Brugge**, **Gent** and **Brussels**. You will pass around Brussels on a ring road, just keep to the right all the time and you will not go wrong. There are numerous motorway services on route which not only serve petrol but also have good facilities for eating, drinking and resting. After Brussels take the **E411** to **Namur**, at junction/exit 18 turn off onto **N4** marked **Bastogne**.

This will take you all the way there. Just before entering Bastogne, about two miles out, you will skirt past on the left the village of MANDE ST ETIENNE, it was around here that the 101st Airborne Division detrucked and went into an assembly area before moving into Bastogne proper. To the right a little further on is SENONCHAMPS, the site of American artillery positions during the siege.

Move on into Bastogne on the **N4**. You will cross over the disused railway line, the original bridge was blown by the retreating Belgian army during the German Blitzkrieg in May 1940. It was rebuilt by the Germans, damaged again during the 1944 siege, and finally a modern structure spans the area. One of the famous landmarks of Bastogne was the water tower. Unfortunately it remains no more, but the base can still be seen about 200 yards before the bridge on the right. Cross the bridge, (Route du Marche). There is rather a good little hotel on the right called Hotel Du Sud. Not much to look at, but it is very reasonable, good breakfast, clean room and free parking.

See potos on page 100.

Passing on a little further on the left is HOTEL LEBRUN, this was the headquarters of Colonel Roberts of CCB 10th Armored

STREET PLAN BASTOGNE

N30 to Houffalize

6

7

Cemetery

N874 to Clervaux

Rue De Marche

Church

1

3

2

N4

4

Rue de Wiltz

8

To Wiltz

Rue De Neufchateau

5

To Assenois

N4

To Arlon

1. Hotel Lebrun
2. Place McAuliffe (car park)
3. Site of Water Tower
4. Au Pays d'Ardenne Museum
5. Bunker
6. Heintz Barrack
7. Mardasson Memorial and museum
8. Tank turret and memorial to fir GI killed in are

Division. Another 200 yards will bring you into the town square called 'Place McAuliffe.' There is plenty of parking, but it is pay and display (10 Bfc per one half hour).

In the square is a tourist office (closed Mondays), which will supply maps, postcards, details of accommodation etc. As you will see, surrounding the square, is an abundance of restaurants and bars. Very much geared up for the tourist, there is even one bar called 'Le Nuts.' The whole place thrives on that few days in 1944.

At the southern edge of the square is an M4 Sherman tank, still showing the damage it sustained during the battle. Alongside the tank is a bust of General McAuliffe and a *Voie de la Liberté* marker. These markers stretch the distance of the route taken by the Allies from the Normandy landings right down to here in Bastogne.

Make your way on foot down the **N85**, marked to Neufchateau. This road is called Rue de Neufchateau, about 100 yards on the left hand side at Number 20 is the Au Pays d'Ardennes museum. Well worth a visit, it contains an insight to military and civil life in Bastogne during the battle, as well as a vast collection of animals and nature with local crafts and tools. Something for everyone. For

The Hotel Le Brun, Bastogne. Command Post of the 10th Armored Division in December 1944.

the enthusiast there are military artifacts for sale at museum – all found locally.

Walk back to the square and proceed down the Houffalize-Clervaux road and turn left, leading to the northwest part of town. Pass under a railway bridge and about a quarter of a mile will be found the HEINTZ ARMY BARRACKS. As you will see, it is still very much in use by the Army, so you will not be allowed in. In 1944 General Middleton had his headquarters within these barracks, and so did General McAuliffe when Middleton moved out.

Sherman tank in Place McAuliffe, Bastogne, showing battle damage.

CAR TOUR ONE

The first suggested car excursion will take a full day to cover all the items of interest.

From the square in Bastogne take the **N85** Neufchateau road, past the museum, and note the monument on the right-hand side just before the bridge carrying the **N4** above you. It marks the spot where a GI named Ernest Glessener destroyed a German tank before being killed himself. He became the first GI killed in the area 10 September 1944, some three months prior to the German offensive and the Battle of the Bulge.

Also alongside the monument is a Sherman tank turret, these will be found on all the main entrance roads to Bastogne and mark the limits of the defence perimeter. Pass under the bridge, **turn right** showing a small sign for Bastogne and Industrial Estate. This brings you out onto the **N4**, after a short distance **turn right again** onto a small road, heading for Assenois.

See page
123 About one mile past the industrial units on the left is a small grove of pine trees also on the left. In amongst the trees is a small bunker. It still bears the scars from the three 75mm shells that were fired from Lieutenant Boggess's Sherman tank. On the side of the bunker is a plaque commemorating the link up between the 101st Airborne Division and the 4th Armored Division. From here you can drive down into the village of ASSENOIS. However, like most of the villages surrounding Bastogne, it has been rebuilt and there is very little to see from the war.

Tank turrets mark the perimeter on all the main roads leading into Bastogne.

ICI AU SOIR DU 26-12-1944
LA 4ÈME D.B (3ÈME ARMÉE U.S GENERAL PATTON)
A REJOINT LA 101ÈME AIRBORNE
ROMPANT AINSI L'ENCERCLEMENT DE BASTOGNE

HERE IN THE EVENING OF DEC 26 1944
4 TH.A.D OF PATTON'S 3D.ARMY
MET WITH 101ST AIRBORNE DVN
THUS BREAKING THE ENCIRCLEMENT OF BASTOGNE

DON
FRATERNELLE GENERAL PATTON IIÈME BAT FUS.
GIFT

HOMM...
AU LT CHARLE...
1911 +
DONT LE CH...
LE PREMIER. L'E...
DE BAST...
SES AMIS A...
ET BEL...

The German bunker on the road to Assenois.

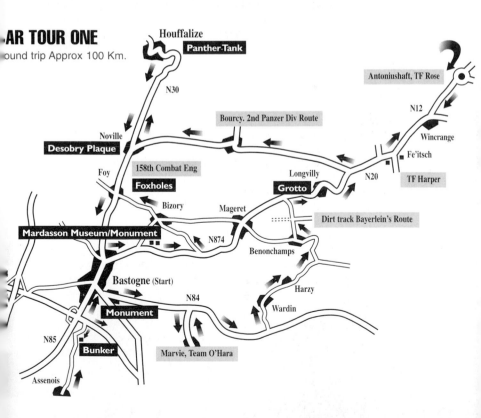

AR TOUR ONE
ound trip Approx 100 Km.

Houffalize
Panther Tank
N30
Antoniushaft, TF Rose
N12
Bourcy. 2nd Panzer Div Route
Wincrange
Noville
Fe'itsch
Desobry Plaque
158th Combat Eng
Longvilly
N20
TF Harper
Foy
Foxholes
Grotto
Bizory
Mageret
Dirt track Bayerlein's Route
Mardasson Museum/Monument
N874
Benonchamps
Bastogne (Start)
Harzy
N84
Monument
Wardin
N85
Bunker
Marvie, Team O'Hara
Assenois

See
page 95
Back to Bastogne and out again, this time on the **N84**, marked Ettelbruck and Wiltz. After about one mile, just before the tank turret marker, turn right for MARVIE. It was in this village area that the 2nd Battalion 327th Glider Infantry had their headquarters and marked the south-eastern portion of the perimeter. Drive back up onto the **N84** turn right and drive for about three miles, **turn lef**t on the **N821** for **Wardin**.

Team O'Hara from the 10th Armored Division was in position just south of this village on the **N84**. Wardin became fiercely contested

See
page 71
over and it was not until 16 January 1945, that it finally fell into American hands. Most of the village was destroyed. Pass through Wardin, still on the **N821**, a very pretty drive will take you through Harzy, turn left to BENONCHAMPS, where the road climbs steeply. In the village take what looks like a reasonable **farm road** on the

See
page 56
right. At the top of the hill a hedgerow on the right can be seen concealing a small partially made up road. To your left it peters out into a mere dirt track. This was the road from NIEDERWAMPACH, that Bayerlein used to get to MAGERET.

Carry on along the twisting farm road past a large quarry and onto the **N874**. Turn **right** for LONGVILLY. After about half a mile

See
page 58
there is a forest on the left and on the right dug into the side of a steep bank is the GROTTO of ST MICHAEL. This was the scene of the head on clash with the German forces and Team Cherry on 18 December. There is parking on both sides of the road. Evidence of the heavy fighting around here can be seen by the bullet spattered rocks.

Drive into LONGVILLY (another village which has been rebuilt). Here, opposite the church in a large house, Gilbreth from CCR 9th Armored Division had his headquarters. Pass through the village, the next turning on the left heads for the village of BOURCY. This was the road that the 2nd Panzer Division took to by-pass north of Bastogne. Stay on the **N874** and **cross the frontier** into Luxembourg where the road now becomes the **N20**. This brings you to a junction where the **N20** meets the **N12**. Opposite is a filling station. The junction here was the spot of the southerly road block (Feitsch) held by Task Force Harper of CCR 9th Armored Division.

See
page 53
Turn left onto the **N12** (signposted Clervaux). Pass through WINCRANGE to the small hamlet of ANTONIUSHAFT. The old junction is now a modern roundabout, but it marks the area of Task Force Rose's roadblock. Do a complete orbit of the roundabout and

See
page 52
retrace your route back down the **N12**, cross the border again and **t**urn right for BOURCY. In the village there are still some buildings that show the scars of battle. Through the village and follow signs

See
page 70
for NOVILLE. At the main junction in NOVILLE, there is a church on the left and on the opposite side of the road is a wall, below the street sign 'Rue Du General Desobry' is a memorial plaque

Battle damage still evident today to a house in Bourcy.

Two views of the German Panther tank at Houffalize.

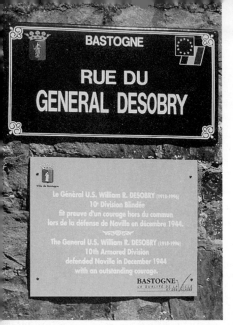

Plaque on the wall at the Noville crossroads, remembering Task Force Desobry 10th AD.

dedicted to Team Desobry of the CCB 10th Armored Division.

From here turn right and drive the six or seven miles to HOUFFALIZE. A very pretty town with lots of restaurants, bars etc and a rather nice German Panther tank, which is worth a look at. This is a good place for a break, and a recharge of your batteries ready for the next onslaught. **Return** along the road out of the town of HOUFFALIZE **(N30)** through NOVILLE and onto FOY; pass through FOY and a little way along the road is a patch of woods on the left. Tank destroyers from Company C 705th Tank Destroyer Battalion were in position here by midnight 18 December.

See pag 68

Return to Bastogne. In the town centre take the Clervaux road **(N874)** again in order to visit the MARDASSON Museum and Memorial. The turning left is immediately after yet another tank turret and is clearly marked. MARDASSON is the name of the hill that the monument is built on. There is a large car park with full disabled facilities available. There

The Memorial at the Mardasson Centre.

A German Hetzer tank destroyer at the Mardasson Centre.

are toilets both in the car park and within the Historical Centre. I
believe there is also a cafe in the car park but it is probably only
open during the holiday season. The Historical Centre is based on
an American five-pointed star. It contains both American and
German uniforms and equipment. The two life size dioramas
featuring German and American scenes are excellent. In the centre
is an amphitheatre in which you can follow the siege quite clearly.
Also there is a cinema regularly showing archive footage from the
battle. Alongside the centre is the inevitable souvenir shop, selling
just about anything that 'Nuts' or 'Bastogne' could be printed,
painted or stamped on.

Price of entry is Bfc 295 per adult, cheaper for children and large
parties. Outside the centre are three armoured vehicles, a
Sherman tank, M10 tank destroyer and a German tank destroyer
(Jagdpanzer).

A short walk over to the memorial will also reveal it is in the
shape of an American star. Around the top are the names of all the
states which make up the Union. Along with colourful names and
insignia of all the US Army and USAAF units which served within
the Ardennes region. It is possible to climb to the top of the
memorial where there is a walkway giving a spectacular view of the
surrounding area. Mind you, it is very high, so if you are nervous of
heights be careful, there is not much of a high surround to keep you
from falling.

An M4 (105mm) Sherman tank at the Mardasson Centre.

The memorial was built for all the US troops who died, were wounded or missing, not just for the battle of Bastogne, but for the whole Ardennes campaign. It was inaugurated on 4 July 1950, by General McAuliffe himself, and other dignitaries, and was built by Mr Calay a native master builder from Belgium.

MARDASSON marks the closest spot that the Germans got to Bastogne from the east.

**See
page 51**

From the MARDASSON centre **turn left** onto the **N874** and just after the hamlet of NEFFE turned **left** for BIZORY or if preferable carry on into MAGERET then turn **left** for BIZORY. After BIZORY the road climbs back towards FOY passing through a fir forest. On both sides of the road, in the forest, there is ample evidence of the fighting. Foxholes and rusting metal fragments are all around. This is where the 158th Combat Engineers Battalion dug in on a line from FOY down to NEFFE.

As previously stated, it is extremely difficult to do a complete orbital guide of the area without having to double back on yourself, such is the road network. Also it is quite a large battlefield to try and take in. Once a certain spot has been reached there is very little else to see but a monument of some description. So badly was the area battered that most of the villages have been completely rebuilt.

Here I must put in a word of warning, if you happen to be walking through the woods and forests in the area, there is a

chance you might stumble across live munitions still lying about. Please do not touch. No matter how rusty and inert they may look, the danger is still there. The area has been very much cleared but there is still the risk that something has been missed. TAKE CARE!

The next tour will take us into Luxembourg to see the route the Germans came.

An unexploded mortar bomb.

Rusting German helmet in the woods at Bourcy.

Artillery artifacts. A lifting eye from a U.S. 105mm shell, and a top of a powder charge container.

Rusting rifle bullets alongside the road near Longvilly.

Statue of an American Soldier in Clervaux.

CAR TOUR TWO

Exit Bastogne on the now well travelled road to CLERVAUX, cross into Luxembourg and descend from the north into the picturesque, fairyland-type town of CLERVAUX. On entering the town the HOTEL CLAVARELLIS is on the right. Proceed into the town centre. There are two car parks directly under the Chateau. They are pay and display and will cost Bfc 20 per hour (If they are working).

See pag 32

Climb the steps to the Chateau, in the outer courtyard is a Sherman tank and a German PAK 88mm field gun. In the inner courtyard, where the 28th Infantry Division held their last stand in Clervaux, is a plaque on the wall. Also a small but very good museum, open daily 1300 – 1700. I rate this as one of the best. In the main square next to the River Clerf is a statue of an American GI.

See pag 47

Back to the car and out of Clervaux via the MARNACH road. You will pass the treble switch back before climbing the steep hill out of the town. There are several view points on the climb to take good photographs of the town and Chateau. At the top is a restaurant, it was close by here that the tanks met head on leaving a crippled MK IV Panzer blocking the approach road to the town from the direction of MARNACH.

See pag 44

Into MARNACH, there is a memorial in the centre, stones with

TOUR GUIDE TWO

Round trip Approx 100 Km.

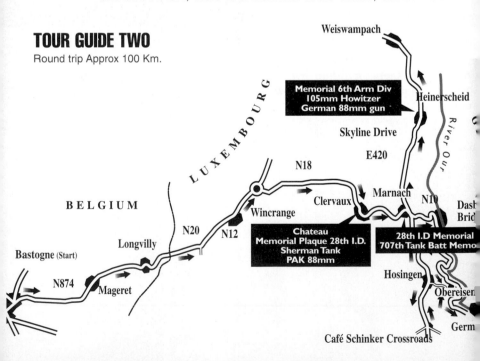

Courtyard Clervaux Chateau.

A plaque commemorating the U.S 28th Infantry Division's stand in Clervaux Castle.

German 88mm field gun in the grounds of Clervaux Castle.

IN HONOR
OF THE BRAVE MEN OF HQ COMPANY,
110th INFANTRY REGIMENT, 28th INFANTRY DIVISION,
WHO HELD THIS CASTLE
AGAINST SUPERIOR GERMAN FORCES
FROM 16 TO 18 DECEMBER 1944
CEBA

German 88mm PAK gun in Heinerscheid.

See
pages
38-40
plaques dedicated to the US 28th Infantry Division and its attached 707th Tank Battalion. Take turning right out of MARNACH marked DIEKIRCH. On to what was then called 'SKYLINE DRIVE,' now almost a motorway.

It was called 'Skyline Drive' because it was the highest road running north to south along the front, consequently, anything on it could be observed from the German positions across the valley.
See
page
34
Turn **first left** marked DASBURG. Proceed down into the valley of the Our River by means of a very steep twisty road. This will bring you to the River Our and the bridge at DASBURG which crosses into Germany proper. It was here that Manteuffel personally directed traffic of the 2nd Panzer Division. **Turn south** on the Luxembourg side and follow the narrow road which parallels the
See
page
30
River to GEMÜND. This area is where the 26th Volksgrenadier Division threw a bridge across and also crossed in boats in the early hours of the 16 December. Panzer Lehr also came across the Our at this point. Although, of course, the bridge, like the one at DASBURG, is new, it is built on the same spot.

Turn around and retrace your steps and **turn left** in the village of OBEREISENBACH for HOSINGEN. In the centre of the town is a
See
page
45
large stone memorial to Georges Boos (some local dignitary I suppose).

A large water tower can be seen (new of course), but in the same

154

position as the one that used to be here in 1944. This was used as an observation post by infantrymen of the US 28th Infantry Division during the attack. It's a good vantage point and Germany across the valley can be seen clearly.

Turn left in town, down 'Skyline Drive' **(N7)** straight across large roundabout on the Diekirch road. After about half a mile a crossroads will be reached. This was the CAFE SCHINCKER CROSSROADS around which the small platoon from the 28th I.D's 110th Regiment held so bravely, watching Germans swarm either side of them as they attacked up from the River Our valley. See page 39

Drive back up 'Skyline Drive' and pass through HOSINGEN, MARNACH and follow signs for ST VITH. At the town of HEINERSCHEID, immediately in front of the church on the right, surrounded by a hedge, is a memorial to the US 6th Armored Division, who later recaptured this area. Also, beside the memorial are two rather nicely preserved field guns. One is a German 88mm and the other a US 105mm Howitzer. This about brings you to the end of this area tour covered by the book. See page 44

US 105 Howitzer in Heinerscheid.

There are many little villages mentioned within the battle equally as famous as the ones I have guided you to. These can be visited by deviating from my route at anytime, to guide you to all of them would mean alot of 'retracing your steps.' So I will leave it up to the individual.

Also, as I have previously stated, all these villages were virtually destroyed during the battle and therefore have been rebuilt, which means they may not take the same form as they did in 1944.

If you follow north out of HEINERSCHEID you will come to the town of WEISWAMPACH just inside Luxembourg. Here are several good supermarkets and filling stations. It is worth bearing in mind that Luxembourg is very cheap for petrol, cigarettes and drink. So before heading back to Belgium, stock up here.

But above all, whilst out touring these villages and battle scenes please try and cast your mind back to those dark days of December, 1944 and try and imagine what those poor brave men of both sides had to endure and contend with.

Enjoy your visit.

Evidence of foxholes dug by the Engineers fifty years ago during the defence of Bastogne.

INDEX